STRIKING GOLD

THE PENGUINS' AMAZING RUN TO THE 2016 STANLEY CUP

This book is available in quantity at special discounts for your group or organization.
For further information, contact:

Triumph Books LLC
814 North Franklin Street
Chicago, Illinois 60610
Phone: (312) 337-0747
www.triumphbooks.com

Printed in U.S.A.
ISBN: 978-1-62937-220-4

Pittsburgh Post-Gazette
John Robinson Block, Co-publisher and Editor-in-Chief
David M. Shribman, Executive Editor and Vice-President
Susan L. Smith, Managing Editor
Mila Sanina, Deputy Managing Editor

BOOK EDITORS
Michael Sanserino, Assistant Managing Editor, Sports
Tyler Batiste, Sports Editor
Alex Iniguez, Associate Sports Editor

PHOTO EDITOR
Andrew Rush

ADMINISTRATIVE COORDINATOR
Allison Latcheran, Senior Marketing Manager

Content packaged by Mojo Media, Inc.
Jason Hinman: Creative Director
Joe Funk: Editor

Front and back cover photos by Matt Freed/Post-Gazette

Matt Freed/Post-Gazette

CONTENTS

INTRODUCTION

By David Shribman

Sure, we've done this before, and recently. Watched the Steelers march through opponents en route to the Super Bowl. Witnessed the Pirates prevailing in a Wild Card game that was wild beyond expectation, or explanation. Held our breath as the Penguins held onto a lead, and onto a dream. Shoved way too much food in our mouths, mostly from nerves, while the game is on. Burst onto the streets in an ode to joy in black and gold that shook the night. Headed Downtown for the parade a few days later. Heck, we even know the parade route. And remember where we stood in 2009.

But somehow this one was the sweetest yet, or (and who else but Pittsburghers could plausibly make this addendum to the sentence?) at least the sweetest recently.

So this is a meditation on the familiarity of jubilation — and the jubilation of familiarity.

No need to remind anyone holding these pages that this is number IV, an estimable record for a club founded in 1967, the year the Maple Leafs of staid old Toronto last won the Stanley Cup. Put it another way: We here in expansion Pittsburgh have won IV more Stanley Cups since the Torontos — an "original six" club with a storied history seasoned with the names Smythe, Mahovlich, Bower, Horton and Sittler — last won a single one. In a culture where knowledge of Roman numbers has faded, Pittsburghers have unusual numerical literacy.

But has it occurred to any 15-year-old that it is not exactly normal for someone her age to have rooted for her team in three Super Bowls and three Stanley Cup finals — and to have seen her team prevail in four of them? Lots of Stanley Cup finals in Detroit, for example, in the life of that 15-year-old. Three of them. But Super Bowl appearances? None, unless you count Super Bowl XL, which was played in Detroit, but which was won by Pittsburgh. How about our other neighbor, Cleveland? Add up the championship series appearances of all its teams, ever, and you will not need many fingers. No problem fitting rings on thumbs up there on the shores of Lake Erie.

The thing about Pittsburgh and championships is that familiarity has not bred contempt. It has bred jubilation.

That couldn't happen everywhere. Take my first hometown, Boston. We all know that the Red Sox drought lasted 86 years, ending in that remarkable sweep of the St. Louis Cardinals in the 2004 World Series. The Sox added another World Series championship three years later, and of course the Patriots added four Super Bowl wins this century. But the Red Sox victory in 2004 drained the team of perhaps its most valuable asset, its maddening human fallibility, and all those terrific Patriots seasons has bred an efficiency that seems at odds with any definition of lovability.

Here, we have fallibility (for many years its

Penguins owner Mario Lemieux hoists the Stanley Cup after the Penguins defeated the San Jose Sharks in Game 6 of the Stanley Cup Final. (Matt Freed/Post-Gazette)

local synonym was Pirates) but also lovability. We love our Steelers, we love our Penguins. This championship season was special in the way that all love affairs are special. Both involve high hopes, great obstacles, sometimes a sense of betrayal, always a whiff of danger. But anyone who has experienced small-town girls and soft summer nights, city girls who lived up the stair, or blue-blooded girls of independent means, knows that the memories of hiding from the lights on the village green, or perfumed hair that comes undone, never fully fades, nor does the conviction that, as the Sinatra song prescribes in D-minor, this was a very good year.

It was a very good year.

It ended with a titanic clash of sporting icons, two of the great teams of any sport, old-fashioned sixes of the grind-it-out tradition, each team destined to be a modifier for the word Nation, always rendered with an uppercase N. We didn't like to think so during some of those sweaty Shark Tank nights, but gradually it became clear: Those Sharks, our colleagues in the animal kingdom as in the kingdom of sporting greats, in fact are our cousins, coming from a town like ours (for many years an afterthought and then a high-tech behemoth), and swiftly developing a folklore like ours, with an ethic like ours, with a fanbase like ours, though with worse uniforms (enough with the Pacific Teal!) and without the colorful local argot n'at (spare us the talk of the Next Wave). As summer approaches we may grow to admire these Selachimorpha (for that is the zoological superorder in which they are classified), and for their ability to prevail in the shadow of a superorder sort of city in their own state, a condition not unknown in our precincts.

Let's not forget that this year began in the dregs of the standings, where our local heroes seemed destined to dwell for the length of the season — until an inspired change ordered from on high in the management transformed the trolls of the hockey downstairs into the shining upstairs champions of Lord Stanley's loving cup.

Our cup runneth over, again. For this Cup is no demitasse, but verily a bowl—in fact, if you will forgive the phrase, a super bowl, especially so since our forces emerged from a fiery trial that held nary a hint that glory might be in the air, or in the offing.

The rest of the story is amply — artfully, in fact — told in the pages that follow. But what makes this Stanley Cup victory special, or especially sweet, isn't a single play, or a single moment, or a single game. Nor a single figure, for who could choose among Crosby, Malkin, Letang, Lovejoy, Kunitz, Murray … and the rookie Rust, who took them to the final in the last breath of a breathless May?

The story here — soon to be a legend, but one that is true — is the way this team responded to adversity. The most overworked description of the teams of our towne (I'm guilty myself, in the very week I write this) is that they possess a work ethic that matches the city in which they play. This is their greatest example, which is why — with bows to our predecessor teams, to the Chief and the Steel Curtain; to Pronovost and Aps and Schock; to Stargell and Clemente and Wagner and both Waners; to Mean Joe and Bradshaw and Swann; to Lemieux and Barrasso and Coffey and company; to the Immaculate Reception and Mazeroski's blast — this may be our greatest hour. Close to last and then firmly in first, and always first in our hearts, the Penguins are champs again. But champions unlike any other, and not only because they are ours. ∎

Penguins goalie Matt Murray makes his way onto the SAP Center ice before Game 6 of the Stanley Cup Final. (Peter Diana/Post-Gazette)

STANLEY CUP FINAL, GAME 1

MAY 30, 2016 · PITTSBURGH, PENNSYLVANIA
PENGUINS 3, SHARKS 2

TAKING A BIG FIRST STEP

Nick Bonino Scores Late in the Third Period, Then the Penalty-Killers Step up and Thwart a Power Play with 2:09 Left for a Dramatic Win

By Dave Molinari

It was not, Nick Bonino said, his hardest shot.

Not in his career.

Not even in this game.

But it was one of the most important, because it gave the Penguins a 3-2 victory against San Jose in Game 1 of the Stanley Cup final at Consol Energy Center.

· The score was tied, 2-2, when Bonino took a feed from defenseman Kris Letang, who was behind the San Jose goal line, and threw a shot past Sharks goalie Martin Jones at 17:27 of the third period to break a 2-2 tie.

"I kind of found a way to flip it over him," Bonino said.

Whether the Penguins will have right winger Bryan Rust for that game wasn't immediately clear. Rust took a high hit from San Jose's Patrick Marleau early in the third period and adjourned to the dressing room. He returned a few minutes later but, after skating one shift, left the game again.

Penguins coach Mike Sullivan described the check as a "blindside hit to the head" and said Rust is listed as "day-to-day."

Rust, who scored both of the Penguins' goals in their 2-1 victory against Tampa Bay in Game 7 of the Eastern Conference final, opened the scoring against San Jose at 12:46 of the opening period. He chopped a Justin Schultz rebound past Jones for his sixth of the playoffs — the most by a Penguins rookie — and fourth in two-plus games.

Chris Kunitz got the other assist, extending his scoring streak to six games.

The crowd of 18,596 still was celebrating that goal when Conor Sheary took a feed from Sidney Crosby and threw a high shot past Jones from just inside the right dot at 13:48. Sheary's shot, which beat Jones high on the far side, was flawless, but the pass that made the goal possible might have been even better.

Crosby had the puck along the left-wing

Bryan Rust celebrates his goal on Sharks goaltender Martin Jones, the first goal of Game 1 of the Stanley Cup Final. (Matt Freed/Post-Gazette)

boards, then threw a cross-ice, backhand feed onto Sheary's stick in the right circle.

"I just tried to find a soft area on the weak side of the ice, and he obviously saw me and made a great pass," Sheary said.

Those goals were the high points of a period in which the Penguins dominated play, mostly by exploiting their advantage in speed. They ran up a 15-4 edge in shots, which was a fair reflection of how those 20 minutes unfolded.

"I thought that first period was as good as we've looked, as a team," goalie Matt Murray said.

San Jose coach Peter DeBoer had a different perspective on the opening period — "We didn't play our game in the first period," he said "we stood around and watched" — and was infinitely more pleased with the second, when the Sharks tied the score on goals by Tomas Hertl (3:02) and Marleau (18:12).

"We knew they were going to push back," Penguins center Matt Cullen said.

San Jose couldn't shove the Penguins all the way out of the game, however, and they preserved the victory by shutting down the Sharks' lethal power play after Bonino's goal.

"Keeping home ice in the series is going to be huge," Sheary said. "So to come out with a win was very important." ∎

Sharks goaltender Martin Jones makes a save on Sidney Crosby in the third period. The Penguins triumphed over the Sharks, 3-2. (Matt Freed/Post-Gazette)

STANLEY CUP FINAL, GAME 2

JUNE 1, 2016 · PITTSBURGH, PENNSYLVANIA
PENGUINS 2, SHARKS 1, OT

CROSBY'S CALLED SHOT

Sheary Overtime Goal Gives Penguins 2-1 Win, 2-0 Series Lead Vs. Sharks

By Dave Molinari

Carl Hagelin is a pretty sharp guy, and undoubtedly got a quality education at the University of Michigan.

But he didn't need any formal training to grasp the value of the Penguins' 2-1 overtime victory against San Jose in Game 2 of the Stanley Cup final at Consol Energy Center.

Because the difference between having a 2-0 lead in a best-of-seven series — as the Penguins do — and being tied, 1-1, as significant as it is obvious.

"It's very different," Hagelin said. "If we would have lost that game, it wouldn't have been devastating, but it would have been tough."

That possibility was rendered moot at 2:35 of overtime, when Conor Sheary beat Sharks goalie Martin Jones from above the left hash mark for his fourth goal of the playoffs.

Sheary has goals in 10 games this season; the Penguins have won nine of them. This one, though, appears to be the first scripted by center Sidney Crosby.

Before a faceoff in the San Jose end, Crosby told his teammates precisely where they should be, and how they should expect the play to unfold. Crosby's plan began with him controlling the draw against San Jose's Joel Ward.

"He said he was going to win it to me," defenseman Kris Letang said, "And I had to find [Sheary]."

Sheary, meanwhile, was told that Letang "was going to find me in the soft area there."

Good plan. Better execution.

Crosby won the faceoff to Letang, who was at the left point and patiently waited for Sheary to get open.

And when Sheary did, Letang fed the puck to him. The same puck that ended up behind Jones a second or so later.

Sheary's goal resulted in the 11th time in Sharks history that they have started a series 0-2. They lost each of the previous 10.

The Penguins are the 50th team to win the first

Conor Sheary celebrates his game-winning overtime goal with teammates and fans. (Peter Diana/Post-Gazette)

two games of a Cup final. The previous 49 are 44-5.

The Penguins never have trailed in this series and took a 1-0 lead in Game 2 at 8:20 of the second period.

Phil Kessel, perched at the right side of the crease, steered in a Nick Bonino shot for his team-leading 10th goal of the playoffs. Hagelin got the second assist.

Bonino's shot might have sneaked inside the right post, but Kessel chipped it into the net to remove any doubt.

"I think guys are going to give him some crap about that, because it's Phil," Bonino said. "But he can't pass that up.

"You have to whack that in."

Hagelin, who got the other assist on that goal, agreed.

"It's one of those things where the puck is about to go in, but it's low, so if [Kessel] doesn't put it in, who knows if someone dives to get it out," he said.

"So he did the right thing."

That goal figured to be the winner until 15:55 of the third, when Sharks defenseman Justin Braun put a shot off the right goalpost and past goalie Matt Murray.

Braun's goal put the game into overtime, but didn't particularly faze the Penguins.

"When they scored late in the third period, we stayed with our game plan," right winger Patric Hornqvist said.

"If we do that, it's going to be hard to beat us."

And the Sharks are starting to run out of chances to try. ■

After a scoreless first period, Phil Kessel nets the puck in the second. Though the Sharks' Justin Braun tied the game in the third, Conor Sheary's goal handed Pittsburgh a win in overtime. (Matt Freed/Post-Gazette)

STANLEY CUP FINAL, GAME 3

JUNE 4, 2016 · SAN JOSE, CALIFORNIA
SHARKS 3, PENGUINS 2, OT

REVERSAL OF FORTUNES

In a Rare Second Overtime Game in the Title Round, San Jose's Joonas Donskoi Tipped the Scales Against the Penguins

By Dave Molinari

Game 3, the San Jose Sharks figured, was when they would make their stand.

Not that they had much choice.

After dropping Games 1 and 2 of the Stanley Cup final to the Penguins, a loss in Game 3 would pretty much have assured the Sharks of leaving the series as silver-medalists.

After all, just four teams in playoff history have rebounded from a 3-0 deficit to win a best-of-seven series. Toronto, in 1942, is the only club to do it in a Cup final.

So the Sharks' 3-2 overtime victory didn't just slice the Penguins' lead in half; it kept San Jose alive as a viable threat to claim the Cup for the first time in franchise history.

The Penguins have a clear edge heading into Game 4 at the SAP Center — they could lose that game and still have home-ice advantage in what would become a best-of-three — but San Jose's pulse remains strong.

"We're in a good position here still," Penguins center Matt Cullen said. "We need to take care of business in the next one."

Joonas Donskoi of the Sharks assured the suspense would remain in the series when he beat Penguins goalie Matt Murray with a turning shot from low in the left circle at 12:18 of overtime to give San Jose not only a victory, but its first lead of the series.

San Jose forced overtime when Joel Ward beat Murray on an unscreened shot from the top of the slot at 8:48 of the third period, just as a double-minor for high-sticking assessed to Penguins center Nick Bonino expired.

The Penguins had killed Bonino's penalty, which was issued for smacking San Jose's Joe Thornton in the face with his stick, effectively, but that was rendered moot when Ward scored the goal that made it 2-2.

"It [stinks] that they were able to tie it in the third, but I thought we had a strong push back," winger Bryan Rust said. "We played well in overtime, but they got the bounce."

Actually, everyone got the bounce. All night.

The puck hopped around the SAP Center ice like an over-caffeinated Super Ball.

Matt Murray stops a shot by the Sharks' Patrick Marleau. Murray stopped 23 of 26 shots on goal. (Peter Diana/Post-Gazette)

"It was tough ice," Cullen said. "[The puck] was bouncing a lot."

The playing surface didn't do much to impede Penguins defenseman Ben Lovejoy.

He scored their first goal and assisted on their other, when Patric Hornqvist deflected his shot past Sharks goalie Martin Jones with 52.3 seconds left in the second period.

Although Hornqvist put the Penguins in a pretty good spot — they had lost just one game since the start of the regular season when leading after 40 minutes — Ward's goal gave the Sharks the boost they needed to get back into the series.

"It is what it is," Penguins right winger Phil Kessel said. "I thought we played good in stretches,

and they played good in stretches."

The Penguins are 13-2 in playoff series in which they win the first two games, and while the defeat in Game 3 stung, they insist that it won't be an issue when they face the Sharks in Game 4.

"That's what we've been doing really well over the past four months, just putting games behind us, whether we win or lose," Rust said. "And move on to the next one." ∎

STANLEY CUP FINAL, GAME 4

JUNE 6, 2016 · SAN JOSE, CALIFORNIA
PENGUINS 3, SHARKS 1

ON THE LIP OF THE CUP

Evgeni Malkin Scored His First Goal of the Championship Round, and Goaltender Matt Murray Made it Stand up as the Winner

By Dave Molinari

Nobody likes to shoot pucks more than Phil Kessel.

Few guys score more goals than he does, either.

But Kessel's most important shot of these playoffs didn't end up in the net. And it probably wasn't supposed to.

But it did get the Penguins started toward what became a 3-1 victory against San Jose in Game 4 of the Stanley Cup final at SAP Center.

The victory that has given them a 3-1 lead in the series also put them into position to win the fourth Stanley Cup in franchise history.

The Penguins never have played a potential Cup-clincher at home. Their titles in 1991, 1992 and 2009 all were won on the road and on the first opportunity.

The Penguins have lost two games in a row just once in these playoffs and have not dropped three in a row since a 0-4-1 skid in mid-December.

The Penguins stopped their most recent losing streak at one, thanks to a solid team effort that was highlighted by a 23-save effort by rookie goalie Matt Murray and two-point contributions by Kessel and Evgeni Malkin.

They were outshot [24-20] for the first time in 13 games, but played with a lead from the time defenseman Ian Cole scored at 7:36 of the opening period until time expired.

Cole, who had not scored in the previous 104 games, counting regular season and playoffs, put them in front to stay when he threw a Kessel rebound past Sharks goalie Martin Jones.

"I was saving a special one for a special game," Cole said, smiling.

Kessel had shot from the right side, and Jones steered the rebound right where Cole expected it to go.

He anticipated there would be a rebound because the Penguins routinely put the puck

Evgeni Malkin scores against the Sharks in the second period, leading the Penguins to a 3-1 victory. (Peter Diana/Post-Gazette)

on goal with the idea of creating one that can be converted into a scoring chance.

"Maybe he was trying to score, and it ended up that way," Cole said. "But I have to give him the benefit of the doubt and say he saw me and put it over there on purpose."

Although Cole put the Penguins ahead to stay, Malkin — shut out in the first three games against San Jose — scored the winner during a power play at 2:37 of the second, when he set up at the right post and chipped in a feed from Kessel for his first goal in seven games.

Malkin also had assisted on Cole's goal and turned in one of his best showings of the spring.

"You saw tonight how dominant he can be," Cole said.

The Sharks, with predictable desperation, surged during the final 20 minutes, throwing 12 shots at Murray and getting on the scoreboard when Melker Karlsson beat him from inside the left circle at 8:07.

"They pushed hard," center Matt Cullen said.

"We defended hard. It was a heck of a hockey game. It was up and down, and [Murray] was up to the challenge."

Checking-line forward Eric Fehr snuffed any chance of a third consecutive overtime game when he beat Jones from the slot at 17:58 to restore the Penguins' two-goal advantage.

And to move them within one victory away of a championship that seemed unthinkable when 2016 began.

"We know that's the hardest one to win," center Nick Bonino said.

"I'm sure we'll see their best game. And we have to bring ours." ∎

Matt Murray makes a save on Sharks center Chris Tierney in the second period. Murray only allowed one goal of 24 Sharks attempts. (Peter Diana/Post-Gazette)

STANLEY CUP FINAL, GAME 5

JUNE 9, 2016 · PITTSBURGH, PENNSYLVANIA
SHARKS 4, PENGUINS 2

SPOILING THE PARTY
Penguins Drop Game 5 to Sharks, 4-2
By Dave Molinari

It was the game the Penguins wanted to play. Heck, it was the game they felt they needed to play if they were going to clinch the franchise's fourth Stanley Cup.

And they played it.

Just not quite long enough in what became a 4-2 loss to San Jose in Game 5 of the Cup final at Consol Energy Center.

The Sharks' victory pared the Penguins' lead in the series to 3-2.

San Jose scored on two of its first three shots, getting two goals in the first three minutes, then withstood a sustained push by the Penguins, who never managed to catch up after falling behind again late in the opening period.

"Everybody knows that we're a better team than those first five minutes," Penguins defenseman Olli Maatta said. "I think we showed it after."

The Sharks frustrated not only the Penguins, who were attempting to become the first Pittsburgh-based team to win a championship inside the city limits since the 1960 Pirates, but thousands of fans who gathered outside the arena and in Market Square to watch the game on large screens.

Game 5 attracted a crowd of 18,680, a record at Consol Energy Center. The vast majority of those people went home disappointed mostly because of San Jose goalie Martin Jones, who made 44 saves.

"They threw a lot of pucks at the net," Jones said. "That's kind of the way they play."

But it wasn't just the quantity of shots Jones faced. More than a few of them came on high-quality chances.

He made a good save on Phil Kessel from inside the right circle on the Penguins' first shot of the game just over three minutes into the contest — the Sharks already had a 2-0 lead by then — and made probably his best stop with just under five minutes to go in the second period when he rejected Nick Bonino's backhander off a Kessel rebound.

"I kind of made life difficult for myself a couple of times with rebounds," Jones said.

Truth be told, the Penguins made his life

Sidney Crosby has San Jose's Tommy Wingels in a head lock during Game 5. The Sharks topped the Penguins 4-2 to send the series back to San Jose. (Peter Diana/Post-Gazette)

difficult much of the evening, too, as they consistently sent pucks and bodies at him.

"We did a great job of taking the puck to the net," right winger Patric Hornqvist said.

And, for a brief stretch in the first, they did a pretty fair job of putting pucks in the net, too.

Evgeni Malkin cut San Jose's lead to 2-1 with a power-play goal at 4:44, and a Bonino shot caromed off Carl Hagelin and into the net behind Jones 22 seconds later to pull the Penguins even.

Nearly 55 minutes remained, but that was the final puck that eluded Jones.

"We couldn't seem to find that third goal," Penguins coach Mike Sullivan said.

San Jose did at 14:47 of the first, when Melker Karlsson beat Penguins goalie Matt Murray — who stopped just four of seven shots in that period — from the left hash mark for what proved to be the winner.

The Penguins continued to control play for much of regulation, but San Jose got the only other goal when Joe Pavelski closed out the scoring with an empty-netter at 18:40 of the third.

And so the Penguins will fly back to California today, and try to get the final victory they need Sunday.

"We just have to bear down," Maatta said. "We had those chances. It just wasn't our day." ■

Sharks goalie Martin Jones deflects a pass by the Penguins' Justin Schultz in the first period. Jones had 44 saves in Game 5. (Matt Freed/Post-Gazette)

STANLEY CUP FINAL, GAME 6

JUNE 12, 2016 · SAN JOSE, CALIFORNIA
PENGUINS 3, SHARKS 1

CHAMPS!

Letang, Dumoulin Break Through Against Brilliant San Jose Goalie Jones, Hornqvist Adds Empty-Netter to Kick Off City-Wide Celebration

By Dave Molinari

Sure, talent matters.

More than just about anything, probably. So a team whose payroll is studded with the likes of Sidney Crosby, Evgeni Malkin, Phil Kessel and Kris Letang, among others, almost has an almost unfair advantage.

But it takes commitment to forge a champion, as the Penguins proved again in the third period of their 3-1 victory against San Jose in Game 6 of the Stanley Cup final at SAP Center.

The victory secured the team's fourth championship and, in the process, etched June 12, 2016, alongside the most celebrated dates in franchise history.

Right next to May 25, 1991, June 1, 1992, and June 12, 2009, when they won their first three Cups.

Just as Crosby scrawled his name beside that of Mario Lemieux (1991, 1992) and Malkin (2009) as the Penguins' winners of the Conn Smythe Trophy as playoff MVP.

But Crosby's receipt of the Smythe — to say nothing of the outcome of Game 6 — was far from certain after 40 minutes.

The Penguins had a 2-1 lead on goals by Brian Dumoulin (yes, that Brian Dumoulin) and Letang, but they knew the Sharks were just one shot from tying the score.

And San Jose got that shot.

Singular.

Unfortunately for the Sharks, Penguins goalie Matt Murray stopped it.

They did not get another until the final minute of regulation, and only after Patric Hornqvist had scored into an empty net at 18:58 to purge any lingering suspense about the outcome.

The commitment the Penguins made to winning a championship couldn't have been more obvious during those first 19 minutes of the third. They blocked shots with every available body part, broke up potential scoring plays by any means necessary.

"That's the type of team we are," left winger Carl Hagelin said. "No one cares about individual

The Penguins celebrate with the Stanley Cup at SAP Center in San Jose after beating the Sharks 3-1 in Game 6. (Matt Freed/Post-Gazette)

stats. We want to get the puck out [of the defensive zone] and do our job."

Murray's teammates all but completely insulated him, effectively eliminating the possibility of the Sharks pulling even by virtue of a bad bounce off the unpredictable SAP Center ice.

"What an effort by a great team," Murray said.

Anything less might not have been enough, because Sharks goalie Martin Jones was sensational again, repeatedly thwarting the likes of Crosby and Kessel on high-quality scoring chances when another goal would have allowed the Penguins to put the game out of reach.

"You have to give Jones a lot of credit," Penguins center Matt Cullen said. "He was outstanding again."

The one obvious flaw in Jones' game is that, like most goalies, he isn't much of a goal-scorer, and the Sharks could have used a few more of those.

As in the first four games of the series, they never led in Game 6.

Dumoulin put the Penguins up, 1-0, with a power-play goal at 8:16 of the first, when he took a cross-ice feed from Justin Schultz, faked a shot to get a clear lane to the net, then pounded the puck past Jones.

Logan Couture got San Jose even at 6:27 of the second, but just 79 seconds later Letang took a feed from Crosby and beat Jones from the bottom of the right circle for what would be the Cup-winner.

Hornqvist's empty-netter sealed the triumphant end to a season highlighted by a coaching change and a significant roster makeover.

"We went through an awful lot," Cullen said. "It was an up-and-down season."

But one in which the Penguins ended up on top.

Because it was all about commitment. ∎

Penguins goalie Matt Murray is mobbed by teammates after Pittsburgh's Game 6 win over San Jose. The win clinched the Penguins' fourth Stanley Cup in franchise history. (Peter Diana/Post-Gazette)

CROSBY CLAIMES CONN SMYTHE TROPHY AS MVP

Penguins' Quiet Leader Plays Instrumental Role in Clincher

By Seth Rorabaugh

Sidelined for virtually the second half of the team's Stanley Cup-clinching victory against the Detroit Red Wings in Joe Louis Arena in 2009, center Sidney Crosby primarily watched his teammates defend their goal from his bench as he dealt with an undislcosed injury.

Seven years to the day of that victory in Detroit, Crosby helped secure the franchise's fourth Stanley Cup championship and in the process, won the Conn Smythe Trophy as the most valuable player of the postseason.

"He's been awesome," said defenseman Olli Maatta. "He's the main leader. He carries this team. When he's on, everybody follows him. That's the main reason, I think, we won."

Crosby was instrumental on the team's final two goals of a 3-1 win at SAP Center.

Only 1:19 after the Sharks tied the score, 1-1, the Penguins regained a 2-1 lead at 7:46 of the second period. Working the puck deep on the left wing, defenseman Kris Letang backhanded it into a pile of bodies in front of the cage. Penguins center Sidney Crosby was able to dig the puck out of the crease, veer behind the net and feed a pass

to Letang, now position to the right of the crease. Letang lifted a wrister which clanked into the net off the inside of Jones' blocker. Crosby and left winger Conor Sheary netted assists.

The Sharks spent the rest of the game trying to force a tie and pulled goaltender Martin Jones late in regulation for the benefit of an extra attacker. Crosby helped set up right winger Patric Hornqvist for an empty-net goal with 1:02 left in regulation. Crosby had the lone assist.

He had 19:41 of ice time on 29 shifts in Game 6. In the third period, Crosby logged 6:41 of ice time on 12 shifts and even saw some time on a key penalty kill in the period.

Accused by Sharks center Logan Couture of cheating on faceoffs after Game 2, Crosby dominated the circle in Game 6 by going 13 for 17 (76 percent) including two wins in as many faceoffs against Couture.

"He does things quietly," said general manager Jim Rutherford. "He's really a great leader.

"Everybody judges Sid on his points and how many goals he gets and things like that. But he's really an all-around player. He plays in all zones on the rink. He plays hard. He leads his team. He leads

NHL commissioner Gary Bettman presents Penguins captain Sidney Crosby with the Conn Smythe Trophy after Game 6.
(Matt Freed/Post-Gazette)

by example and he does things quietly. He's a quiet leader but a really good one."

The award is determined by a vote among members of the Professional Hockey Writers Association.

He is the third Penguins player to claim the award. Centers Mario Lemieux (1991 and 1992) and Evgeni Malkin (2009) preceded him.

Crosby, 28, finished the postseason with 19 points (six goals, 13 assists) in 24 games, sixth in the NHL and second on the Penguins to right winger Phil Kessel (22 points in 24 games).

The award punctuated a postseason for Crosby that saw him finish with a team-leading three game-winning goals. ■

ROAD TO
THE CUP

81

Forward

PHIL KESSEL

Kessel Trade Will Determine Rutherford's Legacy as Penguins GM

By Gene Collier • July 2, 2015

No truth — absolutely none — to this story that the Toronto Maple Leafs had no choice but to trade Phil Kessel because they could no longer afford both his $8 million salary and the extra baggage fees the airlines were charging to get him from one NHL city to the next.

Maybe you've heard Kessel comes with a lot of baggage, the contemporary working term for off-field or off-ice issues, but that doesn't mean much unless it comes with some specifics.

Does the newest Penguin and the centerpiece of the convulsive nine-player trade with the Maple Leafs come with the kind of carrier-approved baggage that fits easily in the overhead bin or safely under the seat in front of you, metaphorically speaking, or is it of the oversized, overstuffed variety that has been out of his possession and possibly augmented by materials from persons not known to him?

"I don't have any concerns," said Penguins general manager Jim Rutherford in a Fifth Avenue bunker hours after he'd acquired the one goal-scorer in the trade market he coveted above all others. "Everybody gets a fresh start in a new place.

You always hear stories about different people in different situations, but I feel very comfortable with getting Phil.

"I've done a lot of homework on this and I've talked to a lot of people. I do believe that getting a fresh start, getting out of Toronto, where he went under the microscope from day one, he was always the guy, the guy that got blamed when things weren't going well, and he doesn't have to be the guy here. We have a bunch of them."

So that's the working premise for the trade that likely will define Rutherford's tenure, that the marvelously talented Kessel, a classical NHL blend of speed and snipery, quickly will observe that there's no smoking on the Penguins bench, and no yawning either, and perhaps discover that a recommitment to conditioning could make his future so much brighter than his recent past.

It was Boston Bruins coach Claude Julien who bought Kessel his first satchel, mentioning not too long after the Bruins made Kessel the fifth player taken in the draft that the young Wisconsinite's interest in defense wasn't terribly robust and that neither was he particularly over-trained.

That didn't stop the Maple Leafs from

Phil Kessel celebrates his goal during the Penguins' 3-2 overtime win over the Capitals in Game 2 of the Eastern Conference Semifinal. During the regular season, Kessel recorded 26 goals and 33 assists. (Peter Diana/Post-Gazette)

acquiring Kessel for three draft picks, one of which turned out to be named Tyler Seguin, and then signing him first to a five-year deal that averaged $5.4 million, then to an eight-year extension that averaged $8 million.

Thus the microscope.

But on Rutherford's team, Kessel will be just one of the five guys who happen to be eating half the cap space (the Penguins will be responsible for a reported $6.75 million annually), so the drop in pressure should be invigorating.

Skating on the right wing next to Sidney Crosby or Evgeni Malkin should make Kessel a 30-goal scorer again or even a 40-goal man, and, if that happens and it accompanies a Penguins return to postseason relevance, July 1, 2015, will write itself into the better history of the franchise.

If that doesn't happen, Rutherford might be skewered for overpayment, although the package the Penguins sent Toronto isn't all that attractive from this view, particularly since Rutherford sealed it without including coveted defenseman Derrick Pouliot.

Essentially, Rutherford got a whole lot of something for a whole lot of maybe, if not a whole lot of nothin'.

The unspoken truth is that the trade will live or die on what Rutherford's more conspicuous superstars demand of Kessel, if anything. Universally described as a highly useful component in a franchise's machinery rather than a born leader, Kessel doesn't necessarily suffer in comparison to Crosby and Malkin on that count.

Sid and Geno are ostensible leaders around here, and not a lot more.

Naturally, the franchise would disagree.

"Sid's the captain of our team; he's the leader of our team," Rutherford said. "On top of that, from the first day that I got here [last spring] to this offseason, I really feel strong about how Sid has taken that role as captain and leader and about where he'd like to see this team go."

With Kessel aboard and Sid and Geno in their primes, the reasons are far fewer today as to why the Penguins can't go and play hockey into June of 2016.

But like the airlines, they'll probably continue to insist on less baggage. ∎

Phil Kessel's shot is blocked by Capitals goaltender Braden Holtby in Game 5 of the Eastern Conference Semifinal. (Matt Freed/Post-Gazette)

JOHNSTON HOPES TEAM CAN CHANNEL FRUSTRATION ON ICE

Closed-Door Meeting Follows Ugliest Loss of Season

By Jenn Menendez • November 17, 2015

Evgeni Malkin clarified his remarks. Sidney Crosby shared his translation. And coach Mike Johnston said he was glad players were mad. He was too.

The Penguins attempted to move forward, 48 hours after a closed-door, players-only meeting capped the team's ugliest night of the season in New Jersey.

Players insisted there is no divide in the room, but that a clearing of the air was needed to shake off an 0-2 slide where effort was called into question.

"Some stuff had to be said. That's got to stay between the players," said veteran winger Pascal Dupuis.

"That's why it's a closed-door meeting. It's between the players. It's unacceptable to lose the way we did. Obviously, we've got to make sure it doesn't happen again."

Malkin told reporters after the closed-door meeting that teammates were "mad at each other." He said they needed to stop, look in the mirror and start working harder. Later, he clarified those thoughts.

"It's little bit not what I want to say. It's not mad at each other. We're a pretty tight team," Malkin said. "We started getting frustrated with each other."

Crosby said the "mad at each other" part of his remarks was lost in translation.

"I talked to [Malkin]. I think the way it was taken was much different than what he meant to say. If you're talking about him saying guys are mad at each other, I don't think guys are mad at each other," Crosby said. "That's not the impression I get. I think guys are frustrated that we're not doing better. It doesn't mean that we're mad at each other or there's a divide in the room."

Whether that's spin or truth, there's been plenty to be mad about. The Penguins sit in fifth place of the Metropolitan Division with a 10-7 record, which in and of itself is not the problem.

It's the unsettling vibe that a team loaded with offensive talent is just not playing or producing at a level at which it is capable.

The club is scoring well below their expected output, with a 27th-ranked 2.06 goals per game. The power play has been lifeless at times, clicking at a 12.3 percent rate, good for a 29th NHL ranking.

In the loss to the Columbus Blue Jackets, only five shots were attempted during six power plays. In the following game, just four shots were attempted

David Perron celebrates his goal against the Minnesota Wild on November 17. The Penguins won 4-3 in their first game after a closed-door, players-only meeting following a loss to New Jersey. (Peter Diana/Post-Gazette)

on three power players.

Goalie Marc-Andre Fleury is having another banner stretch to his career, and it's fair to question if the record would be as good without him.

Johnston said he had no problem with Malkin's remarks.

"He was speaking sort of from his heart, sort of instinctual after the game," Johnston said. "You know guys were mad. I was mad. Our coaching staff was mad. Nobody liked the game we played. It was not a good game and there was no reason for it. … Our effort went down as the game went along. And that's unacceptable. That can't happen."

And in fact, he said challenging one another is important if the Penguins wants to recover.

"Speaking from the heart, you like players that do that," Johnston said. "Sometimes people wade cautiously in the media scrums, but Geno, he's an emotional type of guy like that. … I'm glad players were upset. I'm glad they maybe even challenged each other. As a group that's what we have to do if we really want to function at the highest level."

Crosby said the team does feel the weight of expectations, but he views it as a good thing.

"I think that we all believe in one another and ultimately we all feel the same," Crosby said. "We're all frustrated. We feel we can do better. The expectations are high. I don't see that being a bad thing. We have a winning record and a lot of teams wouldn't put the pressure on themselves to do better and I think we do. And that's a good thing.

"I think a lot of guys care and I think everyone in here is willing to do what it takes to be better but we have to do it consistently and I think it starts with our work ethic. Just establishing that and things will come after that." ∎

Marc-Andre Fleury makes a save on a shot by Minnesota's Brett Bulmer on November 17. (Peter Diana/Post-Gazette)

9

Forward

PASCAL DUPUIS

Dupuis Retires as a Player, but the Penguins Surely Will Find Him a Spot
By Ron Cook • December 9, 2015

Pascal Dupuis is the most emotional sports figure in this town since Jim Leyland. He never has been afraid to cry, never been afraid to show how much he cares about his sport and his team. I still can see his tears a day after the Boston Bruins swept the Penguins out of the 2013 Eastern Conference final. He thought he was going to have to leave as a free agent. I still can see his dismay in November 2014 when he announced he was done for the season and, likely, his career because of an ongoing problem with blood clots.

But there were no public tears from Dupuis, his voice showing just the slightest hint of cracking when he talked of telling his teammates he was done playing hockey. Dupuis had made it back this season to play in 18 games, but he knew it was time to give up the fight. The chest pains he felt Dec. 1 in San Jose, forcing him to leave a game after two periods, made that clear. It was the same pain he felt when he was diagnosed with the blood clots, not just last November but also in January 2014,

a few weeks after knee surgery ended his 2013-14 season after 39 games.

"For me, listening to the doctors is never easy, telling me that I can't do something," Dupuis said before making his comeback this season. "I've been told my whole life that I can't do this or that and I've tried to prove people wrong. But now it's life. These are doctors, not doubters. That's a big difference. The doctors are way smarter than I am."

The docs cleared Dupuis to come back this season and thought they had found the right combination of meds to keep him safe on the ice. But he had a scare in early November in Edmonton, was hospitalized briefly and missed two games. Then, there were the chest pains in San Jose. Enough was enough.

There won't be a more emotional moment all season than when Dupuis, just back after missing the two games after the Edmonton issue, scored 13 seconds into a win Nov. 11 against the Montreal Canadiens, chipping in a cross-ice pass from longtime linemate and friend, Sidney

Pascal Dupuis skates up the ice against the Hurricanes during a September 22 preseason game. Dupuis retired in December. (Peter Diana/Post-Gazette)

Crosby. Consol Energy Center erupted. So did the Penguins bench.

"It gives you chills," Dupuis said that night.

It was Dupuis' final goal, No. 190 of his 14-year career.

The good news is Dupuis, 36, almost certainly won't leave the Penguins.

Mario Lemieux and Ron Burkle are no fools. They will find a place for Dupuis, who could do anything from coaching or scouting to working in the front office or broadcast booth.

The better news is Dupuis almost certainly won't leave Pittsburgh.

Sure, one reason for those tears after the Boston series was because the Penguins didn't reach their goal of a Stanley Cup. Dupuis had been a big part of that talented team, scoring 20 goals in the lockout-shortened 48-game season and then seven more in the playoffs when the Penguins beat the New York Islanders and Ottawa Senators. They averaged 4.27 goals per game — the highest postseason average in 30 years — before running into the wall that was Bruins goaltender Tuukka Rask.

But a bigger reason for Dupuis' tears was he thought he was going to have to leave.

"Every day, I grocery shop," he said. "I go to Starbucks. I take my kids to the park. I go to their hockey and gymnastics and cheerleading practices. We have great friends here away from hockey. We love it here."

The Penguins kept Dupuis by giving him a four-year, $15 million contract. It was a nice reward for a player who might have been the best bargain in sports. Dupuis was due to make $1.5 million in 2012-13 before the lockout and made $1.5 million the season before when he had a career-best 25 goals. It's easy to think the Penguins would have beaten the New York Rangers each of the past two playoff years if Dupuis had been healthy.

Of course, it didn't hurt Dupuis that Crosby liked having him and Chris Kunitz on his line.

"If there's one guy who has believed in me the most during my career, it's No. 87," Dupuis said.

Dupuis played in games against Los Angeles and Anaheim over the weekend, but quickly realized it wasn't fair to continue to put his family, friends and teammates through that stress. Crosby talked of there being "some relief that he doesn't have to worry about that anymore."

That didn't make Dupuis' announcement any easier on his teammates.

"I'm going to miss him a lot," Crosby said. "He's a great guy."

For the record, Crosby had tears in his eyes. ■

Pascal Dupuis works the puck against Red Wings center Luke Glendening. (Matt Freed/Post-Gazette)

STRUGGLES COST JOHNSTON HIS JOB

Wilkes-Barre's Mike Sullivan Tabbed as Replacement; GM Rutherford Wants Team to 'Compete on a More Consistent Basis'

By Dave Molinari • December 13, 2015

The Penguins made a coaching change. Firing Mike Johnston was not a surprise — and arguably was overdue — but simply sliding his nameplate off the head coach's door and slipping Mike Sullivan's in won't be enough to right the Penguins after their wobbly start.

Not unless Sullivan can get guys with big paychecks and bigger reputations — Sidney Crosby, Phil Kessel, et al. — to begin generating goals and points at their customary pace. Unless Sullivan can reboot a power play that is imposing on paper but routinely ineffective on the ice. And, perhaps most important, unless Sullivan can introduce increased accountability among his players.

That means rewarding — or punishing — personnel based on performance, not personal histories; creating an atmosphere in which uninspired showings are not tolerated, rather than being dismissed with a tired excuse or explanation; and accepting nothing less than the very best from what should be a pretty good team.

General manager Jim Rutherford, who made the decision to fire Johnston and assistant coach Gary Agnew, acknowledged that the Penguins' intangibles often have failed to measure up to their talent.

"I want to see this team compete on a more consistent basis, from the start of the game to the end of the game, from game-to-game," he said.

Rutherford made one other move, installing Jacques Martin an assistant coach who will work behind the bench rather than in the press box.

The Penguins are 15-10-3, and sit outside the top eight in the Eastern Conference. They haven't quite lost visual contact with first-place Washington in the Metropolitan Division, but neither must they strain to see teams anchored in the depths of the Metropolitan.

"We're not far from the top of the division," Rutherford said. "But we're not far from the bottom, either."

Rutherford volunteered that, "in fairness to our coach, part of this falls on me" because he did not acquire a puck-moving defenseman who might have coaxed more offense out of Johnston's system.

Still, Rutherford oversaw a major retooling of his lineup in the offseason — bringing in Kessel and solid bottom-six forwards such as Matt Cullen, Eric Fehr and Nick Bonino — and remains convinced this roster is capable of

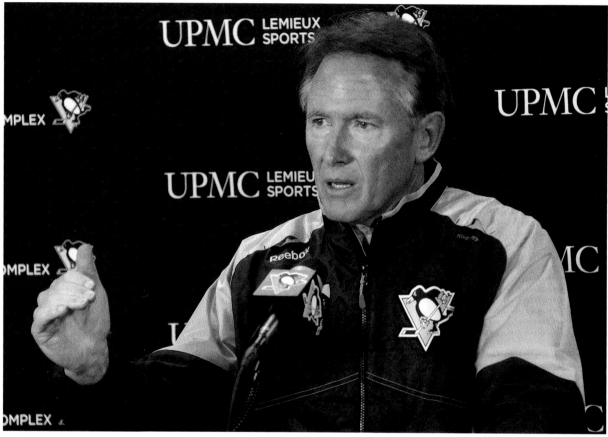

Then-Penguins head coach Mike Johnston talks to reporters during the start of training camp. After a slow start, the Penguins fired Johnston in December. (Matt Freed/Post-Gazette)

contending for a championship.

"We have a group of guys here who I believe have a chance to win a Cup," he said.

Putting Pascal Dupuis and his $3.75 million salary-cap hit on the Long-Term Injured list will give Rutherford the financial latitude to upgrade his roster — "If we can add another player or two prior to the [Feb. 29 trade] deadline, we're going to do that," he said — although there's no guarantee the kind of player he seeks will be available.

One way to enhance the Penguins' skill level on defense without venturing outside the organization would be to promote Derrick Pouliot from their minor league team in Wilkes-Barre. That move figures to be made in the reasonably near future.

Regardless of what happens on their blue line, however, Sullivan must get more offense from prominent forwards in top-six roles; of those, Evgeni Malkin is the only one even flirting with a point-per-game average.

"We have enough offensive players that we should be producing more," Rutherford said.

The onus for that ultimately falls on the players, although Rutherford believes Sullivan's arrival will help.

"You have to have a guy who's going to come in and really take control and deal with some of the guys we need more out of," he said. "We have to pull more out of some guys." ∎

87

Forward

SIDNEY CROSBY

He's Back After Burying the Longest Slump of His Career

By Jenn Menendez • February 10, 2016

When you're the face of the NHL, stretches without goals stand out. Prolonged slumps flash like a neon sign.

And, as games tick by, through October, then November and into December, the whispers around the league multiply, building a crescendo until they are deafening: Is this the beginning of the end for the greatest player in the game?

How utterly ridiculous does that question sound today?

Sidney Crosby, on fire again, is enjoying resurgence on the ice so dramatic that he now has the longest active point streak in the NHL at 11 games. He set a career-long, seven-game goal streak against the Ducks when he scored two breakaway goals, rejoining a scoring race that he wasn't close to being a part of two months ago.

With classic Crosby humility, he will tell you he never went anywhere, that he simply struggled to find his way on the first stretch of his career when the team's scoring chances were dramatically down. His teammates will corroborate this and

stop just short of rolling their eyes with abandon when recalling all that noise.

"We heard about it so much," right winger Patric Hornqvist said. "You know what? Everybody goes through those things in life. Struggle is probably a strong word for it. He was still one of our top players. Maybe he didn't put up points, but he was a leader in the room and on the ice. He stuck with it, played the right way, and now he's gotten rewarded."

Here is Crosby's take. He believes in a very simple lesson he has picked up by playing the game through 10 seasons: Scoring chances are more critical than scoring. One begets the other. Always. It's basic mathematics.

"The biggest thing I've found over the year is chances," he said. "If you're getting chances I feel like it's just a matter of time. If the chances are there, I'm not too worried about the puck going in.

"I think, for the first time, I experienced that there weren't many chances. And, when that doesn't happen, then you've got to find a way to create that confidence in a different way. That was

Sidney Crosby skates up the ice against the Sabres. Crosby finished the regular season with 36 goals and 49 assists. (Peter Diana/Post-Gazette)

probably the biggest thing, creating chances."

Enter a coaching change, some tweaks to the system, and he came alive again.

"I'm not saying confidence is not a part of it, because it is, but I think there's other ways you can get it," Crosby said. "If you're solely looking for confidence in the form of scoring, then, when you're not, what are you going to do out there? You've still got to be effective. I've always felt like I still had an impact even when I wasn't scoring."

His teammates say the finger never should have pointed just at Crosby, that scoring, or the lack of it, was a collective problem.

"From my perspective, it wasn't like this is something that's wrong with him," said Chris Kunitz, Crosby's longtime left winger. "It was something that our team wasn't generating, wasn't scoring. You look up and down the lineup, and the shooting percentage wasn't there. It wasn't there."

Crosby said he can look back and chuckle at some of the theories that emerged. He believes the constant questions were fair — he gets his role. But the speculation raised an eyebrow or two.

"Everyone is entitled to their opinion," Crosby said. "I don't know if I had great answers to be honest with you. I don't think it was the same thing each time I was asked. Game to game it changed. When you're not scoring, you're still searching for ways yourself. I guess the harder part is having to hear other reasons why, when you're searching and everyone else seems to know. … But I understand that's part of it."

His general manager caught his ear a few times along the way.

"I've said it a few times, 'Don't worry about it.' Even when the production wasn't what it's been in past years, he was still playing well," Jim Rutherford said. "Now you look at him, the production is there, he's playing in both ends of the rink. I didn't get a front-row seat over his whole career, but certainly based on what I've seen, he's playing as well as he ever has in his career in all areas of the rink.

"It is impressive to watch, but by no means am I surprised. I've been around the block enough to see how he prepares and how focused he is. This was just a matter of time before the points came."

After a stretch of particularly good games, Crosby took questions from a group of reporters. For a moment, he had the face of a 10-year-old boy, grinning and red-cheeked, just in from a game of pond hockey on a cold winter day.

There was confidence. Joy.

Sidney Crosby was back. ■

Sidney Crosby looks for a pass in the Flyers end. Crosby scored the first goal of the Penguins' 6-2 victory on April 3. (Michael Henninger/Post-Gazette)

JUST IN TIME

It Took Some Changes in Style, Mindset and Personnel, but Penguins Finally Got up to Speed and Found Their Game before Season was Lost

By Jenn Menendez • March 24, 2016

When Penguins goalie Marc-Andre Fleury peers through his mask at his teammates these days, he has a much better view.

The Penguins are not the same Penguins they were in the first half of this season.

They return to the ice tonight against the New Jersey Devils with 88 points, a six-game win streak and a grip on third place in the Metropolitan Division, light years from where they were just a few short months ago.

"It's pretty much the same group of guys. We weren't awful, but maybe fragile is a good word," Fleury said. "It feels better now, for sure."

The Penguins are faster, better in transition and harder to play against. Their confidence appears much harder to shake.

Just ask veteran winger Chris Kunitz, who recalls a team on the edge of the abyss.

The record might have been respectable, but the team's performances were inconsistent, and goal production — along with effort — was sporadic. By late November, the Penguins had reached their bleakest moment, a 4-0 road loss against the Devils that prompted a closed-door meeting and serious soul-searching.

"You go on another losing streak and you're too many points from catching up to even be in the wild-card conversation," Kunitz said. "It has started to turn at the right time of the season. But we're just back in the mix, we haven't separated ourselves. We've just put ourselves back into the conversation."

General manager Jim Rutherford pulled the plug on coach Mike Johnston shortly after that low point and hired Mike Sullivan Dec. 12, which marked the start of the shift.

"It was a gradual process," veteran center Matt Cullen said. "We decided we need to be a lot better team than we are right now. It was, 'All right. What's going to make us successful?' and let's get good at it. We got to work on it, getting pucks out of our end and moving them up ice quickly, and we've continued to work on it every day since."

But there have been some major and notable changes, too.

Justin Schultz celebrates his power play goal against the Capitals on March 20. Pittsburgh won 6-2, the Penguins' sixth win in a row. (Peter Diana/Post-Gazette)

- The addition of defensemen Trevor Daley, Justin Schultz and forward Carl Hagelin, coupled with on-ice adjustments to be faster in transition, have made the Penguins, well, faster.
- The biggest knock in recent postseason losses has been a lack of depth when the big scorers are shut down. But the Penguins have showed legitimate depth from veterans such as Cullen as well as young prospects such as Bryan Rust, Tom Kuhnhackl and Conor Sheary. As a result, they have multiple lines that can produce.
- The coaching change. Johnston was well-respected, but Sullivan is getting through.
- Sidney Crosby is playing like Sidney Crosby. He will take a 12-game point streak into the game tonight and has emerged as a contender for the Hart Trophy with 31 goals, 45 assists for 76 points, third in the NHL before Wednesday.

As a byproduct of those changes and adjustments, the loss of center Evgeni Malkin for 6-8 weeks with an undisclosed injury didn't mark the beginning of the end. Instead, it galvanized the Penguins, who are 5-0 without him.

When Sullivan thinks back to his first days on the job, there is no comparison to where the Penguins are today, especially mentally.

"I think we're in a much different place," he said Wednesday. "From a mindset standpoint, I think we believe that when we play the game the right way, that we're a good team and we can beat anybody.

"The operative phrase is we've got to play the game the right way and every game presents that challenge." ∎

Goalie Marc-Andre Fleury reacts after allowing a goal to the Predators' James Neal on March 31. (Peter Diana/Post-Gazette)

29
Goalie

MARC-ANDRE FLEURY

A Team Man, Family Man

By Ron Cook • April 1, 2016

Marc-Andre Fleury had a relatively easy day at the office. He stopped 22 shots in the Penguins' 5-2 win against the Nashville Predators at Consol Energy Center. It gave Fleury 35 wins for the seventh time in his career. Only legendary goaltender Martin Brodeur has more 35-win seasons in NHL history.

Fleury's real work didn't begin until he went home after the game to his wife and two young daughters.

Now that's a tough job.

Of course, it's also a labor of love.

A new television commercial for Magee-Women's Hospital of UPMC takes viewers into the Fleury home where he, clearly, is a caring, loving father. He uses his goalie glove to change daughter Scarlett's diaper and his hockey stick to push her dirty diaper into the garbage. He later rocks Scarlett and tries to feed her with his water bottle.

"One thing I love about my husband, Marc-Andre, is how he separates hockey from family," Fleury's wife, Veronique, says in the commercial. "Here at home, he's just like any other dad ...

"Well, most of the time."

The spot might not get the national acclaim of Mean Joe Greene's "Coke and a Smile" commercial, but it is absolutely delightful.

"Magee has been great to me and my family. It was easy to do," Fleury said before heading home after this latest win. "But I didn't expect such a big thing around it. Make-up people. Hair people. It was all day. It was almost a 10- or 12-hour day."

The creative advertising people earned their money with the 30-second commercial. They couldn't have picked a better man than Fleury. He is such a natural. His wife does a great job and the kids are adorable, but his personality and smile carry the spot.

"I enjoy it," Fleury said of fatherhood. "It's something you really don't know about until you get into it. It's work, and when you get a second one, it's more work. But when you see them smile and happy, it's priceless."

Fleury's daughters — Estelle, who turns 3 April 26, and Scarlett, 8 months — are too young

Marc-Andre Fleury goes down to the ice during Game 5 of the Eastern Conference Final against Tampa Bay. The 2015-16 season was Fleury's 12th in Pittsburgh. (Matt Freed/Post-Gazette)

to appreciate their dad's hockey greatness. But his teammates certainly do.

The Penguins are expected to give Fleury their highest honor when their Players' Player award is announced. It goes to the teammate they feel best exemplifies leadership and teamwork — on and off the ice. Fleury is among the most respected players in the room and is, without a doubt, the most well-liked. That's why it came as no surprise when he won the Players' Player award last season after Brooks Orpik had won it four years in a row.

"It meant a lot to get that," Fleury said. "Ultimately, I play for the guys in here. We try to help each other do well on and off the ice. You've got to get close. You've got to have good chemistry. I have a lot of respect for them. Guys go through good times, bad times. You battle through it together."

The Penguins' MVP is voted on by the team's players, coaches, front-office executives and just about everyone else in the organization. Fleury said he voted for Sidney Crosby, who is expected to win. "Kris Letang has had a great season, a fantastic season. But I think when Sid turned it on and got going, it got everyone going. That's why we are where we are now."

Second place in the Metropolitan Division — ahead of the New York Rangers, finally — after the win against the Predators.

It was the Penguins' 10th win in 11 games.

Crosby has been terrific, picking up an assist against the Predators that gave him at least one point in 16 of his past 17 games, a total of seven goals, 17 assists and 24 points. He has climbed

into third place in the NHL scoring race and into the conversation for the Hart Trophy, which goes to the league's MVP.

But it's easy to make a strong case that Fleury should win the Penguins' MVP award. He has been their most consistent player all season. He kept the team from falling out of sight in the standings the first two months of the season when Crosby and Letang struggled.

"I've put a lot of time and work into this," Fleury said of his season and his career.

Fleury and his teammates are hoping the best is to come.

They believe they are surging at the perfect time with the playoffs fewer than two weeks away.

Two things seem certain at this point:

One, Fleury will give the Penguins a chance for a deep run. And two, after everything is done, he will go home to his three adoring girls.

They will love him no matter the hockey results. ■

Patric Hornqvist (72) falls on top of goalie Marc-Andre Fleury during a power play drill at Penguins training camp. (Bob Donaldson/Post-Gazette)

ACHES AND PAINS

Injury Woes Have yet to Slow Down Impressive Late-Season Surge

By Jenn Menendez • April 5, 2016

The Penguins have been dealt some heavy roster blows this season.

First came the devastating news that Evgeni Malkin would be out for 6-8 weeks with an undisclosed injury.

Hearts sank around Western Pennsylvania. The Penguins hardly missed a beat.

Next, defensemen Olli Maatta went down, then forwards Scott Wilson, Bryan Rust and defenseman Brian Dumoulin.

Uninterrupted, the Penguins continued a steady climb up the standings.

This past weekend, goalie Marc-Andre Fleury was diagnosed with a second concussion of the season, an ailment notorious for stealing time from a player's career.

Yet the Penguins continued to roll up wins.

Is there a more sure sign that a true team has come together? With the 2016 Penguins, it seems, the whole is greater than the sum of its single parts.

"It definitely shows a lot from the guys in here," winger Eric Fehr said. "But to be honest it's not really talked about too much. We almost assume guys are going to come in and step up. We're a focused group right now."

The Penguins' latest run — wins in 12 of their past 13 — has positioned them favorably for the chance to earn home ice when the Stanley Cup Playoffs begin in little more than a week, to say nothing of marking them as the hottest team in the NHL. The magic number for home ice is four.

General manager Jim Rutherford, chalks it all up to building organizational depth, and a room buying in to its coach.

"At the start of the season we wanted to build a team with more depth," Rutherford said. "That was part of signing extra center icemen and acquiring more defensemen. Then we were also fortunate that we had a group of young guys that were pretty much through their development period and ready to come into the league."

Of all the injured players mentioned above, only Dumoulin has returned to the lineup.

Still, not every group could weather such losses. He must be proud?

"Yeah I am. I'm very proud of these guys and coaches. They've worked hard," Rutherford said. "It takes everyone committing to one the direction for the coach. And that's what these guys have done. And this is the results."

Defenseman Ian Cole said he views his team's ability to keep moving forward despite losing key figures, as a sign of a real team.

"Yeah. I really do. I really think it is," Cole

Marc-Andre Fleury jumps to make a save in front of Islanders Frans Nielsen and Ryan Strome. Fleury suffered his second concussion of the season in early April. (Matt Freed/Post-Gazette)

said. "I just think we're extremely deep, extremely talented in the way that we can continue to play the same that we want to play regardless of who's in the lineup. Everyone knows what they need to do. Everyone knows their job. Everyone knows their role and they execute very, very well."

Cole suspects the resiliency the team has shown could come in very handy in the second season.

"That's a great sign going forward. The playoffs are nasty," Cole said. "You're inevitably going to lose guys, so I think the ability to continue to play a solid team game and have guys step in, who were call-ups, or a healthy scratch, a goalie down in the minors.

"All of these guys have stepped up and have really lead us to where we are and will continue to go where we want to go which is hopefully a better team game and play for a few months here." ■

Head Coach

MIKE SULLIVAN

'Straightforward' Leader Turned Around Penguins Season

By Jenn Menendez • April 15, 2016

Consol Energy Center was electric for the Penguins' 5-2 win against the New York Rangers that opened the Stanley Cup playoffs with a serious bang.

When the puck dropped shortly after 8 p.m., there, amid the noise and energy and pulsating yellow strobe lights, stood the Penguins coach, arms crossed, poker-faced and so sure of himself that, for a moment, it was hard to believe that it had been such a long a time coming for Mike Sullivan.

Before Game 1, Sullivan last led a team into the Stanley Cup playoffs as head coach 12 years ago in Boston — a vast swath of time that could smother the drive of a less determined man.

"To have an opportunity to coach this team has been a privilege," Sullivan said on the morning of Game 1. "To coach in this league is not an easy challenge. There are a lot of really good coaches out there. To have this opportunity for me is a thrill. I'm excited about it. I think our whole team is excited about it."

Sullivan's role in orchestrating a remarkable turnaround has been well documented. He is the man who coaxed the magic back out of Sidney Crosby and Kris Letang, found a way to tap into that relentless team speed and got through to a locker room populated with as many superstars as minor league call-ups. Since his midseason hiring in December, Sullivan has preached a clear message that there is a right way to play the game, and that right way can inspire a run through the postseason no matter who is in the lineup.

"He's an honest guy," winger Patric Hornqvist said. "He tells you if you have a good game or a bad game. Every day. That's what I like."

Back in Boston, those in Sullivan's inner circle never thought it would take this long for "Sully" to get back behind an NHL bench as the boss.

After a 104-point season in Boston, but a quick exit from the 2004 playoffs, Sullivan was shown the door in spring 2006, one year after the lockout.

"I thought he'd be back sooner, to tell you the truth," said Jack Parker, the now-retired and storied coach from Boston University.

Parker coached Sullivan at BU before his NHL career, stole him right out from under crosstown

Penguins head coach Mike Sullivan loses his debut against the Capitals, 3-1, at Consol Energy Center. (Peter Diana/Post-Gazette)

rival Boston College, which appeared to have a lock on the latest prospect from nearby BC High.

Parker saw a cerebral, mature kid who took everything seriously, from hockey to schoolwork.

"It was obvious to me from the get-go when he decided to get into coaching he'd be good at it. There are a lot of guys who can run a drill. He's got the personality and the sincerity to hold people's attention and hold people accountable," Parker said.

That it finally happened for him was music to the ears of John Tortorella, his longtime coaching partner, who said he relied quite heavily on Sullivan during stops in Tampa, New York and Vancouver.

Tortorella said Sullivan was a calming influence on him and a voice of reason. He suspects the playoffs will be his time to shine.

"I know what Sully brings in situations where it may be getting away from you," he said. "The playoffs, where the momentum swings are so important, and maybe things are getting out of hand and you're just beginning to lose yourself as a team. That's where I've learned so much from him."

Tortorella said he knew it was time to let Sullivan go off on his own after Tortorella was fired in Vancouver. Sullivan was getting pigeonholed as a Tortorella sidekick. Job opportunities were literally coming and going.

"He was looked by so many times in the interview process it drove me crazy," Tortorella said.

Still, he said he couldn't help himself and called Sullivan to ask if he would join him in Columbus when he was hired in October. Sullivan said no, and the rest is history.

It didn't start out so pleasant when Sullivan was hired Dec. 12 after two months of coaching the Penguins farm team in Wilkes-Barre/Scranton.

The Penguins were on the edge of sliding out of playoff contention, despite being loaded with star power. Their struggles were perplexing. They seemed fragile.

"We lost four right away, and it would've been pretty easy to start panicking," veteran Matt Cullen said. "But I think his consistency of message and calm throughout the entire thing was really impressive.

"It's one of the things that everybody in here has responded to. He's consistent, very straightforward. It's cut and dry. There's no wiggle room. It's 'This is what I think.' As a player, you respond to that. You know where you stand. You know what's expected of you. For this group, that's been a good thing." ◼

The Penguins finished the regular season 33-16-5 after Mike Sullivan took over as head coach in December. (Matt Freed/Post-Gazette)

30

Goalie

MATT MURRAY

21-Year-Old Rookie Does Not Lack in Confidence, Competitiveness

By Sam Werner • May 13, 2016

When Matt Murray took the ice for his first NHL practice in December, the rookie goaltender was surrounded by a team full of Stanley Cup champions and two former Hart Trophy winners in Sidney Crosby and Evgeni Malkin.

Murray, 21, quickly let all of them know he wasn't intimidated.

"When he was first called up first, up here, he's jamming at guys' feet, whacking at rebounds," defenseman Ian Cole said. "It doesn't matter who it is … he's whacking at guys, trying to clear them out of the crease."

But that competitiveness has fueled Murray's rapid rise in the NHL, where he has emerged as a star between the pipes for the Penguins. He is likely to start in Game 1 of the Eastern Conference final against the Tampa Bay Lightning at Consol Energy Center.

Whether it's in practice or in overtime against the Washington Capitals, the best team in the NHL in the regular season, Murray does not believe any pucks should get past him.

"That's what makes him so good," Penguins goalie Jeff Zatkoff said. "It doesn't matter how it goes in, he doesn't think he should be scored on."

The mindset isn't new for Murray, either. Former NHL winger Lonny Bohonos coached Murray's bantam team for two years in Thunder Bay, Ontario, Murray's hometown.

He recalled a 14-year-old Murray working to prevent every goal he could in practices.

"I think he had that rapport with some of the players," Bohonos said. "If they scored on him, they were pumped."

Bohonos was just getting into coaching when he worked with Murray, so he didn't know what a future NHL goalie looked like as a teenager. But he saw the work ethic and confidence that would serve Murray well down the road.

"Looking back now, am I surprised? By no means," Bohonos said. "No, I'm not. He was good."

Bumps Along the Way

But Murray's rise from teenager to playoff hero was not a straight line.

Matt Murray keeps his eye on the play during the Penguins' 6-2 win over the Philadelphia Flyers on April 3. (Michael Henninger/Post-Gazette)

He was a second-round pick in the major junior Ontario Hockey League's 2010 draft and started his career with the Sault Ste. Marie Greyhounds as a backup in his first year, playing in 28 games.

Murray's second season in the OHL could have been his chance to showcase his skills leading into the NHL draft. Instead, the Greyhounds traded for another goalie, Jack Campbell, a 2010 first-round NHL draft pick, two months into the season.

Campbell and Murray split time that year and, though playing with a former first-round pick might have helped Murray in the long run, it certainly made made his NHL draft outlook a bit murkier.

It also didn't help that Murray's .876 save percentage that year was worst among all OHL goalies who played a significant number of minutes.

That number, though, didn't necessarily concern former Penguins general manager Ray Shero. Yes, Shero admitted, it probably prevented Murray from going in the first round of the 2012 draft, but Murray's 6-foot-4 frame and athletic ability made him more than worth the third-round pick the Penguins used to acquire him.

Still, Shero said the pick was based more on Murray's potential rather than accomplishments.

"You do your due diligence, but it's mostly on projection," said Shero, now the general manager of the New Jersey Devils. "If he can get in the net next year, if two years from now he's the number one goalie there, where could he go?

"The talent, competitiveness, and certainly his size [6 feet 4, 178 pounds]. That was the projection, if he can get in the net at some point over the next couple of years."

Handling Pressure

At the root of all the success was Murray's competitive nature.

"One thing I noticed with Murr last year was just how hard he works in practice," former AHL teammate Taylor Chorney said. "You can just tell, even if it's a rebound in a shooting drill, one that he can't get to because the next guy's coming to shoot, he still gets [ticked] when he gets scored on."

That didn't change when he got to the NHL, either. Murray got his first call-up Dec. 15 and when he didn't see regular playing time right away, made his impact on the practice rink.

"Matty knows everyone believes in him," Zatkoff said. "That's not something that needs to be said."

More importantly than everyone else in the locker room believing in him, though, is the fact that Murray — as always — has supreme belief in himself.

"Confidence is an interesting thing, I guess," Murray said. "I don't think a result should impact your confidence. If you have an outstanding game, that doesn't exactly make you an outstanding goalie. If you have a really bad game, that definitely doesn't make you a really bad goalie." ■

Goaltender Matt Murray makes a save against the Flyers. Murray allowed only 25 goals on 355 shots against him during the regular season. (Michael Henninger/Post-Gazette)

EASTERN CONFERENCE QUARTERFINAL, GAME 1

APRIL 13, 2016 · PITTSBURGH, PENNSYLVANIA
PENGUINS 5, RANGERS 2

AN UNLIKELY HERO

Zatkoff Makes Postseason Debut as Starting Goalie and Muzzles Rangers

By Dave Molinari

A lot of people were shocked when Jeff Zatkoff was the Penguins' starting goalie for Game 1.

Zatkoff wasn't one of them.

He said he "had a pretty good idea" the night before that he would be filling in for Marc-Andre Fleury, who is recovering from a concussion.

And Zatkoff made the most of having time to prepare, stopping 35 shots to lead the Penguins to a 5-2 victory against the New York Rangers at Consol Energy Center in Game 1 of their opening-round playoff series.

"He was probably our best player," right winger Patric Hornqvist said. "The first 10 or 15 minutes, he made three or four really good saves to keep it 0-0. If they get it to 1-0, it's probably a [different] game."

The Rangers didn't get the first goal, and Zatkoff, who made his Stanley Cup playoffs debut, never allowed them to have a lead.

Strong as his performance was, Zatkoff had to share top billing with Hornqvist, who recorded his first career playoff hat trick.

"It was a good night for me," Hornqvist said.

But possibly a better one for Zatkoff. He got the call because Fleury did not dress for the game despite participating in the morning skate, while backup Matt Murray is out with an unspecified injury.

Before replacing Murray in the regular-season finale in Philadelphia, Zatkoff had not played since Feb. 20, but there was no rust evident on his game against the Rangers.

That's mostly because he spent countless hours — before, during and after practices — preparing for an opportunity there was no guarantee ever would come.

"You can't predict what's going to happen," Zatkoff said. "Just make sure you stay ready and control what you can control."

What he couldn't control was the defensive effort of his teammates, but they came through in a big way, blocking 22 shots and limiting New York's second-chance opportunities.

"Our guys made a lot of blocks before pucks got to the net," Zatkoff said. "I was able to find the ones that made it through, for the most part."

While Fleury was absent from the start, New York only had its go-to goalie, Henrik Lundqvist, for the first 20 minutes.

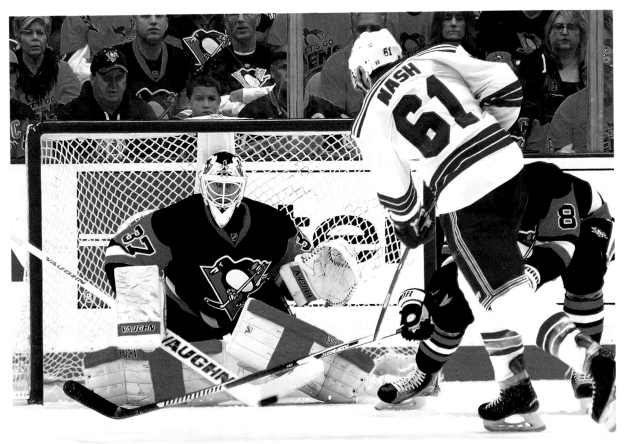

Penguins goalie Jeff Zatkoff makes a save on a shot by the Rangers' Rick Nash in the third period. Zatkoff had 35 saves in the Penguins' 5-2 win. (Peter Diana/Post-Gazette)

Late in the first period, he was struck in or near the eye by the stick of Rangers defenseman Marc Staal and was replaced by Antti Raanta for the final two periods.

Rangers coach Alain Vigneault said Lundqvist will be re-examined.

About a half-minute after Lundqvist was hurt, Hornqvist put a shot between his legs to give the Penguins a lead they never relinquished.

Although they were being outshot, 12-3, at one point — "Obviously, our first period was not as good as we wanted," Hornqvist said — Zatkoff kept New York from scoring.

Hornqvist sprung Sidney Crosby on a breakaway that led to the Penguins' second goal at 18:56 of the second and, after Derek Stepan ruined

Zatkoff's shutout bid at 3:10 of the third, Tom Kuhnhackl scored a short-handed goal that proved to be the winner at 5:31.

Hornqvist added a power-play goal at 8:02 and, after Stepan struck again at 10:11, closed out the scoring with an empty-netter at 17:10.

That secured Zatkoff's first career playoff victory and helped to make an enduring memory for him, as the crowd saluted him late in regulation by chanting his name.

"That sent chills through me a little bit," Zatkoff said.

"That's exciting. … It's fun getting the job done at home in front of your fans.

"It's a special moment. It's one I'll always remember." ∎

EASTERN CONFERENCE QUARTERFINAL, GAME 2

APRIL 16, 2016 • PITTSBURGH, PENNSYLVANIA
RANGERS 4, PENGUINS 2

A DOSE OF REALITY

Focus, Home Ice Advantage Lost in Game 2

By Dave Molinari

This is not an unfamiliar situation for the Penguins.

That doesn't necessarily mean it's a comfortable one.

It is the third time in as many years that they've split the first two games of a best-of-seven playoff series with the New York Rangers.

They lost both of the previous series.

But the mathematical implications of the Rangers' 4-2 victory at Consol Energy Center might not be as troubling as how the Penguins lost Game 2 — with poor decision-making and worse execution, particularly in a five-minute stretch in the second period.

During that time, a 1-0 lead morphed into a 3-1 deficit, as New York scored two goals in 18 seconds and three in a span of four minutes, 18 seconds.

"We had probably a five- or six-minute span in the second period where we lost some of the details of our game, the awareness away from the puck," coach Mike Sullivan said.

"When our team is at its best, we've been defending really well. A couple of the goals were uncharacteristic of this group."

The Penguins were beaten despite regaining the services of Evgeni Malkin, who hadn't played since March 11 because of an undisclosed injury.

He logged 18:47 of ice time and picked up an assist on the second of Phil Kessel's two power-play goals. He centered a line for Bryan Rust, who returned after being out since March 29, and Conor Sheary and also worked at left wing alongside Sidney Crosby.

Goalie Marc-Andre Fleury (concussion) had been considered a possibility to play, but was scratched for the second time in the series.

His replacement, Jeff Zatkoff, stopped 24 of 28 shots and produced several quality saves, most notably on breakaways by Derek Stepan and Rick Nash.

"I felt comfortable in there," Zatkoff said. "Obviously, I would have liked to have made a couple more saves."

Zatkoff's counterpart, Rangers goalie Henrik Lundqvist, made 29. He had been struck in the right eye by the stick of teammate Marc Staal late in the first period in Game 1, but showed no effects of that injury.

"He's an elite goaltender," Rangers coach Alain Vigneault said. "A big-game goaltender."

Penguins goalie Jeff Zatkoff stopped 24 of 28 shots against the Rangers in Game 2. (Peter Diana/Post-Gazette)

Lundqvist's biggest stop might have come with about 4 ½ minutes left in the second. New York had taken a 2-1 lead on goals 18 seconds apart by Keith Yandle and Derick Brassard just a few minutes earlier, when Rust finished serving a minor penalty and got a breakaway.

Lundqvist stopped him.

"I didn't really put my shot where I wanted to," Rust said. "He read me well and played it well, so give him all the credit in the world.

"It was a little bit of a momentum-changer. It would have been nice if I would have scored."

Especially when, little more than a minute later, Mats Zuccarello beat Zatkoff from the inner edge of the right circle for the game-winner. Chris Kreider converted a Trevor Daley turnover into a

goal 39 seconds into the third period to put New York up, 4-1, but the issue had been settled before the second intermission.

"The last five minutes of the second period, we lost focus," Malkin said. "It's the playoffs. You need to play [well] all 60 minutes."

The Penguins, who have relinquished home-ice advantage, will have a chance to do that in Game 3 at Madison Square Garden.

"It's playoff hockey," Daley said. "Every game is so important. You have to move on to the next one." ∎

EASTERN CONFERENCE QUARTERFINAL, GAME 3

APRIL 19, 2016 · NEW YORK, NEW YORK
PENGUINS 3, RANGERS 1

CULLEN UNLOCKS THE DOOR

Breakaway Goal in Third Period Gives Penguins 2-1 Lead in Series

By Dave Molinari

Matt Cullen has been around this game for a long time.

Occasionally, that probably makes him feel really old, like a guy who could have been claimed in the expansion draft.

The one that resulted in the league growing to the Original Six.

But there are other times when all that experience Cullen has accumulated has a tangible payoff, when he executes a heady play that can be traced to the many years he has spent in rinks.

Like the goal Cullen scored to make the Penguins' 3-1 victory against the New York Rangers at Madison Square Garden possible.

Although he has gotten several key goals this season, this was the biggest, for it has given the Penguins a 2-1 lead in their opening-round playoff series.

The victory restored the home-ice advantage they relinquished with a loss in Game 2.

And while Cullen wasn't the Penguins' only hero in this game — rookie goalie Matt Murray, making his first Stanley Cup start, turned aside 16 of 17 shots during his first game action in 10 days — no one had a greater impact.

The score was tied, 1-1, early in the third period when Cullen carried the puck across the New York blue line.

As he approached the Rangers' defense pairing of Keith Yandle and Dan Boyle, Cullen nudged it past them.

Those two nearly collided, and Cullen collected the puck once he got by them, then went to the net and threw a wrist shot past Rangers goalie Henrik Lundqvist for what proved to be the winning goal.

"The puck was kind of bouncing a lot tonight," Cullen said. "It was kind of a tough puck for [Yandle and Boyle] to play. I was just kind of in the right place at the right time."

Yeah. Funny how often that seems to happen for a guy who's 39 years old and undecided about whether to extend his career beyond the spring.

If Cullen does retire, it won't be because his teammates don't appreciate how he has performed this season.

"He's been doing it all year," center Sidney Crosby said. "Especially down the stretch, you can look at a number of games where he gets clutch goals. … That was a big play for him, to get us that lead."

Murray was something of a surprise starter,

Matt Cullen's breakaway goal on Rangers goalie Henrik Lundqvist in the third period proved to be the game-winning goal in Game 3. (AP Images)

having participated in practice the previous day for the first time in more than a week, but the layoff didn't show. He seemed as composed as ever from the start of the game, and wasn't fazed when Rick Nash gave New York a 1-0 lead with a short-handed goal 39 seconds into the second period.

"He played really well," Cullen said. "It was fun to see how calm and composed he was. He looked so big in the net, and I think our whole team fed off that."

Whatever the Penguins were grazing on, the coaching staff might want to include it in every team meal.

They limited the Rangers to 17 shots on goal, including just four in the third period.

Aside from a quirky power-play sequence that led to Nash's goal, the Penguins had few glaring defensive lapses.

"At least in the third period, we didn't give them anything," right winger Patric Hornqvist said. "We were always on the right side of the puck. … They couldn't get their speed going. That's exactly how we have to play when we get a lead."

Even with all his experience, Cullen couldn't have said it any better. ▪

EASTERN CONFERENCE QUARTERFINAL, GAME 4

APRIL 21, 2016 · NEW YORK, NEW YORK
PENGUINS 5, RANGERS 0

IN THE FAST LANE
Malkin Gets up to Speed with 4-Point Game
By Dave Molinari

The Penguins didn't play a flawless game — no team ever does — but it was close enough to earn them a 5-0 victory against the New York Rangers at Madison Square Garden in Game 4 of their first-round playoff series.

"We won, 5-0, and played our best game of the series, by far," right winger Patric Hornqvist said. "When we play the right way — with a lot of speed — and try to challenge their [defense], we're going to be hard to beat."

Recent history, though, reminds the Penguins that they shouldn't be thinking about their next opponent just yet, for they have lost two of the past three series in which they held a 3-1 lead.

It happened against the Rangers in Round 2 in 2014 and against Tampa Bay in the opening round in 2011.

"For sure, you have to learn from things," said center Sidney Crosby, who missed the Tampa Bay series because of a concussion. "But we're doing good things.

"We know our identity. We know that when we don't have that edge, don't play with that level of desperation, we're not the same team, and we can't

expect the same results."

Of course, it's worth noting that Evgeni Malkin, who had two goals and two assists in Game 4, also missed that Lightning series because of a knee injury.

And after two subpar performances in Games 2 and 3, when he was coming off a five-week absence because of an undisclosed injury, he was downright dominant in Game 4.

"I've started to play a little bit better," Malkin said.

His teammates were a bit more effusive.

"He and Sid can make things happen from nothing," Hornqvist said. "They can take over games. They can take over series."

Rookie goalie Matt Murray looks like he just might be capable of that, too.

When the Penguins imploded against the Rangers two years ago, Murray — who turned aside 31 shots in Game 4 to earn his first Stanley Cup playoffs shutout — was still in junior hockey.

He has started the past two games and allowed a total of one goal.

"He really played fantastic," defenseman Ian Cole said.

So did most of his teammates, especially when

Evgeni Malkin is congratulated by his teammates after scoring his second goal of the night against the Rangers. (AP Images)

there was any suspense about the outcome.

"I thought, for the most part, we were pretty good," forward Eric Fehr said.

Fehr set the tone for the evening 69 seconds after the opening faceoff, when he charged at the New York net and knocked a Ben Lovejoy rebound past Rangers goalie Henrik Lundqvist to give the Penguins a lead they never surrendered.

The Penguins got a power-play goal from Hornqvist and an even-strength score from Conor Sheary before the first intermission, and Malkin chipped in with a man-advantage goal in the second period and another in the third.

Just that quickly, the Penguins moved to within

a victory of Round 2. Not that they expect the Rangers to accept elimination easily.

"It's going to be very hard," Cole said. "They're a very good team."

But the one New York is playing has been better. ■

EASTERN CONFERENCE QUARTERFINAL, GAME 5

APRIL 23, 2016 · PITTSBURGH, PENNSYLVANIA
PENGUINS 6, RANGERS 3

RETURN OF THE GOOD VIBES

Penguins Get Happy Ending to Playoff Trilogy with Rangers

By Dave Molinari

It had been a while since the Penguins were on the sunny side of a handshake line.

Just five days shy of two years had passed since they'd closed out a six-game victory over Columbus in Round 1 of the 2014 playoffs, to be precise.

To the guys who had ended the previous two seasons congratulating the New York Rangers on eliminating them from the Stanley Cup playoffs, it probably seemed longer.

Like, forever.

So when the Penguins clinched a spot in Round 2 with a 6-3 victory against the Rangers in Game 5 of their opening-round series at Consol Energy Center, receiving the well-wishes rather than offering them was particularly satisfying.

"It was fun," defenseman Kris Letang said. "It was fun. That's the only thing I can say about it."

The Penguins knocked off New York in five games, their quickest victory in a series since beating Ottawa in five in Round 2 in 2013.

Ending the Rangers series at the earliest opportunity was critical for the Penguins, on several levels.

Not only because of some troubling history — they'd lost two of the past three series in which they took a 3-1 lead and were just 1-8 the previous nine times they could have closed out a series at home — but because the Rangers have a veteran lineup capable of seizing control if it got momentum stemming from a victory in Game 5.

"We certainly didn't want to have to go back to New York for Game 6," Penguins coach Mike Sullivan said.

The Penguins rendered that issue moot with a dominating performance in the second period.

They entered it with the game tied, 2-2, and left it with a 6-2 lead and their ticket to Round 2 all but officially punched.

"We just played our game," said right winger Phil Kessel, who scored the Penguins' second goal. "We used our speed. The little things. And we got rewarded."

The Penguins got goals from Bryan Rust (two), Matt Cullen and Conor Sheary during the second period.

Rangers goalie Henrik Lundqvist, the key to New York's chances of staging an upset, stopped only eight of 12 shots during those 20 minutes, and was replaced by backup Antti Raanta for the second game in a row.

His rookie counterpart for the Penguins, Matt

Bryan Rust (far right) scores the first of his two goals in Game 5. With the 6-3 win, the Penguins advanced to Round 2 of the Eastern Conference Semifinal. (Peter Diana/Post-Gazette)

Murray, stopped 38 of 41 shots to earn his third victory in the series.

Murray was, as always, unfazed by adversity, including having New York's two first-period goals put into his net by teammates Ben Lovejoy and Patric Hornqvist.

That kind of misfortune might cause some goalies to wonder if it simply wasn't going to be their day.

Murray isn't one of them.

"No," he said.

Then, by way of elaboration, Murray added, "No."

A reasonable response, considering how often he said "No" to the Rangers during the final three games.

Murray is one of 13 players who dressed for Game 5 but weren't in the lineup when they lost Game 5 to the Rangers a year ago.

This team is faster, deeper and much more menacing than the 2015 edition.

"We were not good enough last year," Hornqvist said. "We're a way better team this year."

And they're bracing to face a pretty good one — to say nothing of an arch-rival — in Round 2, whether it's the Capitals or Flyers.

"It doesn't get any easier," center Sidney Crosby said. "That's for sure." ∎

EASTERN CONFERENCE SEMIFINAL, GAME 1

APRIL 28, 2016 • WASHINGTON, D.C.
CAPITALS 4, PENGUINS 3, OT

OVERTIME BLUES CONTINUE

Oshie's Winner Deals Penguins 8th Loss in Row in Playoff OT

By Dave Molinari

The Penguins' lineup is laced with gamebreakers, guys who can end a game with a burst of brilliance.

Perhaps one of them will do it in overtime of a playoff game someday.

It hasn't happened in a long time.

The Penguins' 4-3 loss to Washington in Game 1 of their Eastern Conference semifinal series was their eighth consecutive defeat in a playoff game that extended beyond regulation.

They haven't won one since Brooks Orpik, now with the Capitals, eliminated the New York Islanders with a goal in Game 6 of the first round in 2013.

Only a handful of current Penguins were around for that game, and most are blissfully unaware of the franchise's poor fortune in such games.

"I didn't know that," defenseman Ben Lovejoy said. "It's not something that's on our mind."

Washington's T.J. Oshie sealed their most recent defeat at 9:33 of overtime as he carried the puck around the net and wrapped a shot inside the left post to complete a hat trick. A lengthy video review confirmed that the puck had eluded goalie Matt Murray and crossed the goal line.

Oshie's third goal came on the last of Washington's 35 shots. The Penguins threw 45 at

Capitals goalie Braden Holtby, who turned aside 42.

Each side had stretches in which it enjoyed the better of the play. Each had times when it was on its heels, if not its back.

"This game could have gone either way," Penguins coach Mike Sullivan said. "It was an even game."

Mind you, being down, 1-0, to Washington in a best-of-seven series against the Capitals hardly is new for the Penguins. Although they have won seven of eight previous playoff series against the Capitals, the Penguins have lost the opener to them eight times.

The Penguins also have dropped Game 1 seven consecutive times when opening a series on the road.

Murray's loss was his first in these playoffs and, while it wasn't his strongest performance, he did come through with several quality stops, including a pair of uncontested chances for Capitals left winger Alex Ovechkin.

Murray said, "I was happy with my play," and Sullivan absolved him of any particular responsibility for the defeat.

"I thought he was fine," Sullivan said.

While Murray couldn't necessarily be blamed

With his goal in the second period, Nick Bonino tied the score at 3-3. Washington's T.J. Oshie scored in overtime to give the Capitals a 4-3 win in Game 1. (Peter Diana/Post-Gazette)

for the outcome, the same wasn't true of Oshie, whose fingerprints were all over it.

With the Penguins holding a 2-1 lead midway through the second period on goals 57 seconds apart by Lovejoy and Evgeni Malkin, he picked off an Olli Maatta pass in the Washington end, then carried the puck up the ice before throwing a shot by Murray.

Oshie then put Washington in front, 3-2, at 3:23 of the third by tossing a backhander past Murray from the left circle.

Nick Bonino forced overtime by scoring at 8:42, but that was the final goal by either team until Oshie's winner.

Washington had an 8-6 edge in shots in overtime, which Bonino suggested was a reflection of the Penguins' uncharacteristically cautious approach after regulation.

"We played a little bit back, more than we usually do," he said. "We let them come in on the rush, and that's the way they beat us."

Although the Capitals grabbed the early advantage in the series, nothing in Game 1 suggested it will be anything but the lengthy, fiercely contested best-of-seven so many predicted.

"We'll learn from it, put it behind us," Sullivan said. "And try to get Game 2." ■

EASTERN CONFERENCE SEMIFINAL, GAME 2

APRIL 30, 2016 · WASHINGTON, D.C.
PENGUINS 2, CAPITALS 1

FEHR'S GOAL STUNS OLD TEAM

Gets Winner, Then Rookie Murray Slams Door on Capitals

By Dave Molinari

It is, on the most basic level, simply one victory. It guarantees the Penguins almost nothing, except that they won't be swept by Washington in this second-round playoff series.

But their 2-1 victory against the Capitals in Game 2 also means that the Penguins have avoided falling into a 0-2 hole against a team that had the NHL's best record in the regular season. Fact is, the Penguins have grabbed home-ice advantage in the series.

"It's important, because 0-2 is a little bit harder," center Evgeni Malkin said. "But now we're tied, coming back home."

The Penguins are in that position, at least in part, because of Malkin, who threw the pass that Eric Fehr steered past Washington goalie Braden Holtby at 15:32 of the third period to break a 1-1 tie.

"I just tried to re-direct it," Fehr said. "And, luckily, got enough of it that it went in."

The Penguins played nearly the entire game with five defensemen after Olli Maatta absorbed a late, head-high hit by Washington's Brooks Orpik at 4:13 of the opening period.

Orpik got an interference minor; Maatta, who clearly was dazed, got an assisted trip to the locker room.

There was no immediate word on the nature or severity of Maatta's injury.

While the NHL's Department of Player Safety reviews all hits that are even remotely controversial, there was no immediate word on whether Orpik will be hearing from the league.

Maatta's absence forced the Penguins' remaining defensemen to take on heavier workloads. No one assumed a bigger one that Kris Letang, who was on the ice for 33 minutes, 22 seconds.

"It's tough, especially when you're a team that wants to play fast and get your [defensemen] in the rush," Letang said. "I think we did a great job."

Despite the void Maatta's absence created on

Chris Kunitz (left) leaps for joy after assisting Eric Fehr on the game-winning goal against the Capitals. (Peter Diana/Post-Gazette)

their blue line, the Penguins limited Washington to 24 shots on goal, including just five in each of the first two periods.

The Capitals didn't get their first on goalie Matt Murray in the second period until 14:47, but ratcheted up their attack during the third, when he faced 14.

Washington managed to get one by him — Marcus Johansson punched in a loose puck during a power play at 4:08 of the third — but Murray came up with several game-saving stops shortly before Fehr scored.

He denied Alex Ovechkin from in front with just over seven minutes left in regulation, then rejected an Andre Burakovsky backhander about a half-minute later. Thirty or so seconds later, Mike Richards missed the net from directly in front of it.

"There were parts of the game when they took over, and we were sitting back and Murray made some huge saves for us," Fehr said.

The Penguins never trailed in Game 2, as Carl Hagelin opened the scoring at 7:08 of the second period, beating Holtby from below the hash marks for his second of the playoffs. Nick Bonino, who fed the puck to Hagelin from behind the goal line, got the assist to give him points in four consecutive games, a career-best in the playoffs.

Having home ice gives the Penguins a nominal upper hand in the series, but Washington has a history of success at Consol Energy Center. That's part of the reason the split of the two games at Verizon Center was critical for the Penguins.

"They're the Presidents' Trophy winners for a reason," Fehr said. "To be able to come into their building, where they were successful all season, and steal one, that's big." ■

Evgeni Malkin is sandwiched by Washington's Tom Wilson and John Carlson in the first period of Game 2. (Peter Diana/Post-Gazette)

EASTERN CONFERENCE SEMIFINAL, GAME 3

MAY 2, 2016 · PITTSBURGH, PENNSYLVANIA
PENGUINS 3, CAPITALS 2

A WELCOME MATT

Rookie Murray Stops 47 Shots; Penguins Seize 2-1 Series Lead

By Dave Molinari

Marc-Andre Fleury was one of the NHL's top goaltenders in the regular season. Might have been the Penguins' best player, too.

Which means they're pretty lucky to have him as their No. 2 guy.

Fleury returned to the lineup after missing a month because of a concussion, but won't get into a game anytime soon if rookie Matt Murray continues to play the way he did in the Penguins' 3-2 victory against Washington in Game 3 of their second-round playoff series at Consol Energy Center.

Murray stopped 47 shots, including the first 35 he faced, to allow the Penguins to grab a 2-1 advantage in this Eastern Conference semifinal series, even though they were severely outplayed by the Capitals.

Murray was named the game's No. 1 star. Probably wouldn't have been a bad idea to give him the Nos. 2 and 3, as well.

"Without him, there's no way we win," right winger Patric Hornqvist said.

Whether Kris Letang, the cornerstone of the Penguins' defense corps, will be on their blue line then remains to be seen. He faces possible discipline from the league after dropping Washington's Marcus Johansson with a hit to the head at 15:41 of the opening period.

Replays appeared to show that Letang's elbow went into Johansson's chest, while his upper arm and/or shoulder struck Johansson in the head.

Johansson went to the Capitals locker room for medical attention but returned for the start of the second period, and Letang received an interference minor.

That's the same penalty Capitals defenseman Brooks Orpik received when he felled Penguins defenseman Olli Maatta with a head-high hit in Game 2.

Orpik served the first game of a three-game suspension.

The NHL's Department of Player Safety, which handed down Orpik's punishment, conducted a preliminary assessment of Letang's hit.

Letang took a hit to the head of his own with about 7 ½ minutes left in the second period. He checked Capitals left winger Alex Ovechkin to the ice, then was smacked in the back of the head by

Rookie goalie Matt Murray is congratulated by Ben Lovejoy after the Penguins' 3-2 victory over the Capitals. (Peter Diana/Post-Gazette)

Washington center Nicklas Backstrom's left leg when Backstrom tried to jump over them.

If the Penguins lose Letang because of a suspension, it would open a gaping void on their defense. He routinely leads them in ice time and logged a team-high 27 minutes, 57 seconds in Game 3.

"Not only does he play that much, but he plays at a world-class level," defenseman Ian Cole said.

The Penguins lost a man early in the game for the second time in three nights.

Game 2, it was Maatta. Game 3, winger Bryan Rust departed after blocking a shot in the first minute.

Coach Mike Sullivan did not have an update on his status for Game 4.

Washington ran up a 49-23 edge in shots that was an accurate reflection of how the game played out.

"The disparity in shots was because they had the puck all night," Sullivan said.

Nonetheless, the Penguins got first-period goals from Hornqvist and Tom Kuhnhackl and one from Carl Hagelin in the second that allowed them to hold off Washington in the third, when Ovechkin and Justin Williams scored.

But while Murray allowed the Penguins to steal the victory, they realize they won't survive the series if they can't elevate their play.

"We can't expect to play like that and continue to win," center Sidney Crosby said. "We know we'd better be much better in Game 4." ■

Rookie goalie Matt Murray stopped 47 shots in the Penguins' Game 3 win over the Capitals. (Peter Diana/Post-Gazette)

EASTERN CONFERENCE SEMIFINAL, GAME 4

MAY 4, 2016 · PITTSBURGH, PENNSYLVANIA
PENGUINS 3, CAPITALS 2, OT

JUST CALL HIM SAINT PATRIC

Hornqvist Nets Winner to End Penguins' OT Skid in Playoffs

By Dave Molinari

Most of the Penguins knew the history. Some had lived it.

And even those who had spent just a few months on the payroll seemed to be aware the franchise had lost eight consecutive overtime games in the playoffs.

They also were convinced that streak would end eventually.

They just couldn't have known it would happen at such an opportune time.

Patric Hornqvist snapped their run of misery by beating Washington goalie Braden Holtby from inside the right circle at 2:34 of overtime to give the Penguins a 3-2 victory at Consol Energy Center in Game 4 of their Eastern Conference semifinals playoff series.

"It's been awhile," center Sidney Crosby said. "But that was definitely a big one."

Quitting has been all the rage in some Washington political circles this week, but the Penguins know the Capitals won't be suspending their campaign for a place in the next round anytime soon.

"We know we have a lot of work left to do," said goalie Matt Murray, who stopped 34 of 36 shots in Game 4.

The Penguins have lost a series in which they held a 3-1 lead as recently as the second round in 2014, so they are unlikely to take a spot in the conference final for granted.

Not when they're facing such an accomplished opponent.

Not when each of the first four games in this series has been decided by a goal.

"We have to have some urgency [in Game 5]," coach Mike Sullivan said. "We have to have a heightened intensity … We have to bring our best to get the result we're looking for."

Hornqvist gave them the result they craved in Game 4 after Washington defenseman Mike Weber, a Cranberry native, took a one-handed swipe at the puck and knocked it across the ice to him.

Matt Cullen celebrates after scoring in the second period. Cullen almost added a second goal in the third period when his shot hit the crossbar. (Peter Diana/Post-Gazette)

"I don't know how it ended up on my stick," Hornqvist said. "When I saw it on my stick, I wanted to shoot it as quick as I can. It went in, and it was a great feeling."

The Penguins played without defenseman Kris Letang, who served a one-game suspension for a head-level hit on Washington's Marcus Johansson in Game 3, and forward Eric Fehr, who has an undisclosed injury.

Justin Schultz replaced Letang in the lineup, while Oskar Sundqvist took Fehr's spot.

The series has been pockmarked with controversial acts, and there were several more in Game 4.

In the second period, Penguins center Evgeni Malkin checked Washington winger Daniel Winnik just inside the Penguins' blue line, knocking him out of the game for a while.

Available replays did not make it clear where the principal point of contact on the hit was.

And about six minutes into the third period, Capitals left winger Alex Ovechkin slashed Crosby, who left the ice and went to the locker room, on the left arm.

"When it initially happened, I didn't think it was good," Crosby said. "I didn't know if I was going to come back."

He returned a few minutes later, and was on the ice when Hornqvist ended the game. And the overtime losing streak.

But not, the Penguins were quick to point out, the series.

"We'll enjoy it for tonight," said center Matt Cullen, who scored the Penguins' second goal. "And then we'll get back to work." ∎

Trevor Daley (center) celebrates after assisting on a goal by Sidney Crosby in the first period. (Peter Diana/Post-Gazette)

EASTERN CONFERENCE SEMIFINAL, GAME 5

MAY 7, 2016 · WASHINGTON, D.C.
CAPITALS 3, PENGUINS 1

VICTIMS OF A POWER SURGE

Give up Two Goals While a Man Down; Holtby Does the Rest

By Dave Molinari

Washington compiled the NHL's finest record in the regular season. It has a power play with enough skill to alter the course of a game in a matter of seconds.

Its goaltender might well have been the league's best at his position in 2015-16.

And, for the first time in this second-round series, all of those things looked the part in the Capitals' 3-1 victory against the Penguins in Game 5 at Verizon Center.

Holtby rejected 30 of 31 shots, including sensational stops on Patric Hornqvist and Justin Schultz from close range late in the second period to preserve Washington's two-goal advantage.

"I think I jumped higher when he made that glove save [on Schultz] than when we scored any of our goals," Capitals forward T.J. Oshie said.

Two of those goals came from Washington's power play, which converted 2 of 5 chances after going 1 for 12 in the previous four games.

"Everybody knows that's a good power play," Penguins center Matt Cullen said. "You play with

fire when you give them too many opportunities."

Washington defenseman Brooks Orpik is eligible to return in that game, having completed a three-game suspension for a hit to the head on Penguins defenseman Olli Maatta in Game 2.

Defenseman Kris Letang, who was suspended for the Penguins' 3-2 overtime victory in Game 4, returned to their lineup for Game 5. So did forward Eric Fehr, who sat out that game because of an undisclosed injury.

Unfortunately for the Penguins, Holtby showed up, too, and in a way he hadn't in any of the previous four games.

Holtby wasn't the reason Washington had gotten into a 3-1 hole, but no one played a bigger role in making sure the Capitals weren't buried in it.

"We had some chances," Penguins right winger Phil Kessel said. "Obviously, he's a good goalie."

Hornqvist, the Penguins' first-line right winger, had scored on Holtby in each of the previous two games, but made it onto the ice only twice in the third period.

Coach Mike Sullivan said Hornqvist was not

Capitals goaltender Braden Holtby, who had 30 saves in Game 5, blocks a shot by Patric Hornqvist in the second period. (Matt Freed/Post-Gazette)

injured, and that he simply went with the players who were performing best.

"We just shortened the bench," Sullivan said.

For the game, Hornqvist played 10 minutes, 36 seconds and was credited with two shots.

Chris Kunitz was the only Penguins player to get a puck past Holtby in this game, knocking in a Kessel rebound from the crease on a power play at 7:08 of the opening period.

Alex Ovechkin got the first of Washington's power-play goals on a shot from the top of the left circle at 4:04 of the first period, and Oshie scored the game-winner on a man-advantage four minutes into the second.

And while Washington's final goal, by Justin Williams at 9:58 of the second, stemmed directly from a Brian Dumoulin giveaway, the Penguins felt their overall performance wasn't bad.

"It's not a matter of us not playing well," Cullen said. "I thought we played real well in a lot of areas, but there were a few spots where we slipped a little bit.

"That's kind of uncharacteristic of us, but that's a good team on the other side, too. They played a good game, they got the breaks and executed on the opportunities they had."

Which is why this series will continue.

And why its outcome remains far from settled. ■

EASTERN CONFERENCE SEMIFINAL, GAME 6

MAY 10, 2016 · PITTSBURGH, PENNSYLVANIA
PENGUINS 4, CAPITALS 3, OT

IT'S JUST IN THE NICK OF TIME

Bonino Scores Series Winner after Washington Rally Forces OT

By Dave Molinari

Phil Kessel has been around this game for a long time and has seen an awful lot.

Heck, he even has been part of a team that squandered a late three-goal lead and lost an elimination game.

But there was a sequence in the Penguins' 4-3 overtime victory against Washington in Game 6 of their Eastern Conference second-round playoff series at Consol Energy Center — a victory that hoisted the Penguins into the Eastern Conference final — unlike anything Kessel ever has witnessed.

Or likely will again.

In a span of 122 seconds midway through the third period, the Penguins — who already had seen a 3-0 lead fade into a 3-2 advantage — were penalized for delay of game no fewer than three times.

"That was pretty crazy, wasn't it?" Kessel said. "I don't think I've ever seen that."

Most people, aside from the standing-room crowd of 18,650 at Consol Energy Center, probably haven't.

But when Chris Kunitz shot a puck over the glass at 10:32, it sparked an epidemic that ran through the Penguins like a flu bug through a kindergarten class.

Nick Bonino, whose rebound goal at 6:32 of overtime would end the series, was sent off for the same offense at 11:38.

And not long after Kunitz left the penalty box, defenseman Ian Cole completed the Penguins hat trick of delay minors, launching yet another puck into the seats.

"It was a little shock, when you see that third one go over [the glass]," Penguins center Sidney Crosby said. "You almost have to laugh sometimes in situations like that. You just have to find a way to get through it."

Before the Penguins got back to full strength, Washington defenseman John Carlson scored a five-on-three goal that forced overtime, but the Penguins were able to regroup, kill an interference minor against defenseman Kris Letang late in

Nick Bonino celebrates after scoring the game- and series-winning goal in overtime. (Peter Diana/Post-Gazette)

regulation and then close out the series on Bonino's second goal of these playoffs.

He scored it by punching a Carl Hagelin rebound past Capitals goalie Braden Holtby.

"It wasn't pretty," Bonino said. "It was the second or third whack at it."

But it got past Holtby and propelled the Penguins into the Eastern final for the first time since Boston swept them in 2013.

The Penguins and Lightning have met in the playoffs once, and the Lightning rallied from a 3-1 deficit to eliminate the Penguins in Round 1 in 2011. Crosby and Evgeni Malkin were injured and did not play in that series.

Kessel, a member of the Toronto team that melted down against Boston in a Game 7 three years ago, staked the Penguins to a 1-0 lead at 5:41 of the opening period, and the Penguins seemed to all but put the game out of reach when Kessel and Hagelin scored power-play goals in a span of 33 seconds in the second.

"Our power play, the last couple of games, came to life," Crosby said.

But so did Washington's, and man-advantage goals by T.J. Oshie at 18:30 of the second and Carlson at 13:01 of the third helped to erase the Penguins' lead.

"They're a good hockey club," Kessel said. "And we knew they were going to push."

The Capitals did, but the Penguins pushed back.

The intermission that followed the third period gave them a chance to refocus, and they took full advantage.

"It was quiet in here," Bonino said. "Not much had to be said."

Not until a little later, when the Penguins had eliminated the Capitals for the eighth time in nine playoff meetings and secured a spot among the NHL's final four.

"We persevered," Kessel said. "And got it done." ∎

Matt Murray makes a save on Washington's Evgeny Kuznetsov in the second period. The Penguins' Game 6 win eliminated the Capitals, sending Pittsburgh on to the Eastern Conference Final against Tampa Bay. (Peter Diana/Post-Gazette)

EASTERN CONFERENCE FINAL, GAME 1

MAY 13, 2016 · PITTSBURGH, PENNSYLVANIA
LIGHTNING 3, PENGUINS 1

LIGHTNING AND THUNDER

Tampa Bay Overcomes Loss of Top Goalie, Stifles Penguins

By Dave Molinari

Andrei Vasilevskiy's name is more than a mouthful.

But while spelling it correctly is a challenge, getting pucks past Vasilevskiy can be even tougher.

It certainly was for the Penguins in their 3-1 loss against Tampa Bay in Game 1 of the Eastern Conference final at Consol Energy Center.

Vasilevskiy, who figured to watch the series from the far end of the bench, was pressed into service when the Lightning's No. 1 goalie, Ben Bishop, was injured in the 13th minute of play.

He responded by stopping 25 of 26 shots.

"I don't think there was much of a drop-off," Penguins goaltender Matt Murray said.

Or any, for that matter.

Of course, it didn't hurt that Vasilevskiy's teammates closed ranks in front of him, neutering the Penguins offense for an extended period after he entered the game.

"We went through a stretch where we outshot them, 11-2, after [Vasilevskiy] came in," Lightning coach Jon Cooper said. "He's got to jump into the lion's den there, and he didn't have to face anything."

Whether Bishop, who was taken off the ice on a stretcher after he appeared to injure his left knee while scrambling back into position on a Penguins flurry, will be able to play when the series resumes isn't clear.

Cooper said Bishop underwent X-rays and that an examination showed "there's nothing structurally wrong" with him.

There were some fundamental flaws, however, in the Penguins' game. Despite outshooting the Lightning, 35-20, they were guilty of letdowns and lapses that turned up immediately on the scoreboard.

Alex Killorn, for example, put Tampa Bay in front to stay when he got behind Penguins defenseman Olli Maatta and pulled in a long pass from Victor Hedman before going to the net and throwing a backhander between Murray's legs at 18:46 of the opening period.

"[Maatta] lets Killorn get behind him on that one, and we would like him not to allow … not to let him get behind him," Penguins coach Mike Sullivan said. "Olli, positionally, could have been in a better position so he wasn't vulnerable."

Ondrej Palat of Tampa Bay made it 2-0 with a power-play goal at 2:33 of the second and

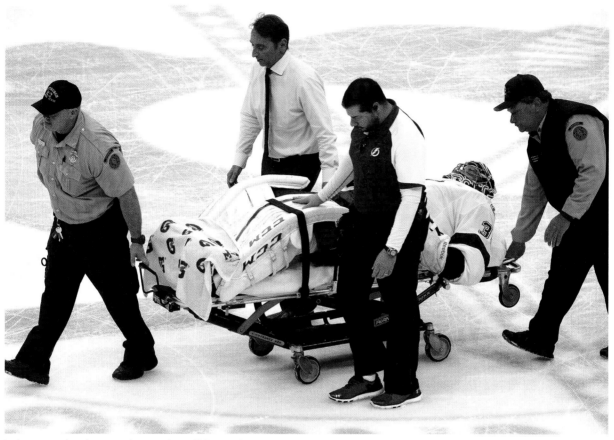

Lightning goaltender Ben Bishop is taken off the ice after getting injured in the first period. Bishop would miss the remainder of the series. (Matt Freed/Post-Gazette)

Jonathan Drouin capped a three-on-one break by beating Murray from inside the right circle at 18:25 of that period.

"Against that team, you can't let your foot off the gas," Penguins center Matt Cullen said.

"If they get an opportunity, they're going to score.

"Their forwards are extremely dynamic and skilled and opportunistic. That's not a secret."

By the time Patric Hornqvist of the Penguins scored a power-play goal at 19:05 of the second, it did little more than spoil Vasilevskiy's chance to share a shutout with Bishop.

"We need to find another level if we're going to beat this team," Hornqvist said.

And they definitely have to avoid spotting the Lightning three-goal leads.

No matter whether Bishop or Vasilevskiy — or No. 3 Kristers Gudlevskis — is in goal, Tampa Bay is committed and stingy defensively.

"They defend hard," Sullivan said. "They block shots. They have people in the [shooting] lanes."

There's every reason to believe Tampa Bay will be doing those same things — and a lot of others — when the series resumes.

The question is whether the Penguins have the talent and the discipline to counter effectively.

They did not in Game 1.

"I don't think it was our best game," Sullivan said. "And that's what we need at this point of the season." ∎

EASTERN CONFERENCE FINAL, GAME 2

MAY 16, 2016 · PITTSBURGH, PENNSYLVANIA
PENGUINS 3, LIGHTNING 2, OT

CROSBY STEALS THE SHOW

Ends Scoring Drought in Style with Goal 40 Seconds into OT

By Dave Molinari

Sidney Crosby's teammates never doubted that they would see him score another goal. They just didn't know that it would take eight games, three periods and 40 seconds for it to happen.

Or that the goal, when it finally came, would be as significant as it was.

Crosby beat Tampa Bay goalie Andrei Vasilevskiy from above the left hash mark 40 seconds into overtime to give the Penguins a 3-2 victory in Game 2 of the Eastern Conference final at Consol Energy Center.

The goal — the fastest overtime winner in franchise playoff history — tied the series, 1-1.

While Tampa Bay surely is satisfied to get a split after playing the first two games on the road, the Penguins are more than a little relieved that they won't have to try to climb out of an 0-2 hole in Tampa.

Perhaps, they are aware that the past 19 teams to lose Games 1 and 2 in a conference final didn't survive the series.

"We definitely didn't want to go down, 2-0," forward Eric Fehr said. "We don't want to split at home, but that's the position we were put in and we're happy with it now."

Crosby rendered his teammates' concerns moot with his fourth goal of the playoffs and first since Game 4 of Round 1 against the New York Rangers.

"I'm just happy, whether I scored in the last seven games or hadn't scored in the last whatever," he said.

Crosby's goal-scoring drought had been a major topic of discussion outside the Penguins locker room, but his co-workers insist they had no fears his scoring touch had deserted him.

"Everybody in this room knew it was just a matter of time," defenseman Ben Lovejoy said. "And he saved a huge one for tonight."

Crosby scored after taking a close-range pass from winger Bryan Rust.

"When a guy like that's yelling at you and he's wide open for a one-timer, you've got to get him the puck," Rust said.

Sidney Crosby looks for room around Lightning sticks in the second period. Crosby later scored the winning goal in overtime. (Matt Freed/Post-Gazette)

The winner came on the Penguins' 41st shot on Vasilevskiy.

"He was outstanding tonight, and probably the reason that game went into overtime in the first place," Lightning coach Jon Cooper said.

Vasilevskiy's counterpart with the Penguins, Matt Murray, struggled a bit early — he allowed two goals in a span of two minutes, 33 seconds late in the opening period — but turned aside all 13 shots he faced in the final 40-plus minutes.

"I was fighting it, definitely, a little bit, especially in the second period," Murray said. "I kind of battled through it mentally and I thought I made a couple of big saves when I needed to."

Murray was particularly displeased about Tampa Bay's second goal, which Jonathan Drouin scored from near the right dot with 49.2 seconds to go in the opening period.

"I think it's fair to say he would have liked that second one back," coach Mike Sullivan said.

Murray, though, was as resilient as he has been throughout these playoffs, purging thoughts of Drouin's goal from his memory almost immediately.

"Matt's a mental rock," Lovejoy said. "He's able to put goals behind him. He does an amazing job at just stopping the next puck."

With Crosby's goal-less streak snapped, attention now will focus on Evgeni Malkin, who doesn't have one in the past seven games.

His co-workers don't expect that slump to last much longer, either.

"Our team has done a good job of having different guys step up every game," Fehr said. "Those guys are always going to be there for us when we need them." ∎

Hitting the ice, Sidney Crosby battles for a loose puck in the first period. (Peter Diana/Post-Gazette)

EASTERN CONFERENCE FINAL, GAME 3

MAY 18, 2016 · TAMPA, FLORIDA
PENGUINS 4, LIGHTNING 2

SHOWER OF STARS AND GOALS

Hagelin's Score Late in Second Period Opens Floodgates

By Dave Molinari

The Penguins probably spent much of the night wondering if they would ever get a puck past Tampa Bay goaltender Andrei Vasilevskiy.

They finally managed to do it, though.

And then they made a habit of it.

Carl Hagelin's rebound goal with 10 seconds left in the second period triggered a burst of offense that gave the Penguins a 4-2 victory against the Lightning in Game 3 of the Eastern Conference final at Amalie Arena.

Tampa Bay controlled the play through the early part of the opening period, running up a 7-2 advantage in shots during the first 7 ½ minutes.

The Penguins, though, generated several quality scoring chances around the middle of the period.

A little more than nine minutes into the game, Vasilevskiy denied Patric Hornqvist twice from the left side of the crease.

Shortly thereafter, he rejected shots from in front by Hagelin and Phil Kessel.

The Lightning had the only power play of the first period, but failed to get a shot on Penguins goalie Matt Murray while Hornqvist was serving a slashing minor assessed at 17:42.

One of the Penguins' best scoring chances came as the period was about to end, when Vasilevskiy stopped a backhander by defenseman Trevor Daley from the right side.

Holding Tampa Bay scoreless in the first 20 minutes was at least a minor moral victory for the Penguins, because it was the first time in nine games that the Lightning didn't get at least one goal on them in the opening period.

The Penguins completely dominated the second period, throwing 21 shots at Vasilevskiy.

And they needed every one to get a puck past him.

Hagelin scored with 10 seconds left before intermission, when he punched in a Kessel

Sidney Crosby and Evgeni Malkin celebrate after Chris Kunitz scored in the third period. A few minutes prior to the Kunitz goal, Crosby had a goal of his own assisted by Malkin and Justin Schultz. (Peter Diana/Post-Gazette)

rebound for his fifth goal of the playoffs.

Vasilevskiy was the primary reason the game was scoreless to that point, as he rejected everything the Penguins threw at him until Hagelin was able to cash in that rebound.

Some of his better stops came on a Sidney Crosby backhander from between the hash marks at 11:23, a Kessel uncontested shot from inside the right circle at 12:22 and an Evgeni Malkin rebound with about six minutes to go.

Murray preserved the Penguins' lead a little more than four minutes into the third period, when he stopped a Brian Boyle shot from the slot, then turned aside J.T. Brown on the rebound.

His teammates rewarded him a minute later, when Kessel took a feed from Nick Bonino and beat Vasilevskiy from the left side of the crease at 5:16.

The goal was Kessel's seventh of these playoffs, but the first he has scored on the road.

The Penguins were still savoring that goal when Tyler Johnson cut their lead in half 14 seconds later. Johnson grabbed a loose puck inside the Penguins' blue line, charged down the slot and beat Murray from just below the right hash mark.

The Penguins nearly got that goal back 38 seconds later, but Crosby couldn't beat Vasilevskiy from the slot. Crosby got revenge on a four-on-three power play at 10:50 as he took a pass from Malkin and drove a shot by Vasilevskiy from just below the right dot for his fifth of the postseason.

Chris Kunitz padded the advantage at 13:12, scoring his second of the playoffs from low in the right circle. Vasilevskiy had made a stellar save on him seconds earlier, but Tampa Bay's Cedric Paquette cleared the puck directly to Kunitz.

Ondrej Palat scored at 18:16 to slice the margin. ■

Bryan Rust battles for the puck in the Penguins' 4-2 win over the Lightning in Game 3. (Peter Diana/Post-Gazette)

EASTERN CONFERENCE FINAL, GAME 4

MAY 20, 2016 • TAMPA, FLORIDA
LIGHTNING 4, PENGUINS 3

TOO BIG A HILL TO CLIMB

Penguins Rally for Three Goals, but Loss Ties Series at 2-2

By Dave Molinari

Losing Game 4 was the easy part.

At least that's how the Penguins made it look for the first two periods of a 4-3 loss against Tampa Bay in Game 4 of the Eastern Conference final at Amalie Arena.

Deciding which goaltender they should use when the series, which is tied, 2-2, shifts back to Consol Energy Center for Game 5 might be considerably tougher.

Coach Mike Sullivan said shortly after Game 4 that "I haven't really given it any thought," and precedent suggests he might not publicly commit to a goalie until game day.

Possibly around game time.

But Marc-Andre Fleury, long the Penguins' franchise goalie, became a viable option when he replaced Matt Murray for the third period and stopped all seven shots he faced in his first game action since getting a concussion March 31.

"There was a little getting used-to in the beginning, but the more it went on, the better I felt," Fleury said.

His teammates seemed to be impressed by what they saw.

"He looked like Flower," center Sidney Crosby said.

Game 4 might not be all the Penguins lost, because defenseman Trevor Daley left the game after appearing to injure his left knee or leg when Tampa Bay's Ryan Callahan checked him into the boards from behind at 10:43 of the second period.

Sullivan said he did not have information on the nature or severity of Daley's injury after the game, but readily acknowledged his value.

"He's a hard guy to replace," Sullivan said. "He plays a lot of minutes. He plays in key situations."

Murray made his 13th consecutive start, but was replaced after allowing four goals on 30 shots.

He hardly was the primary culprit for the Penguins' defeat — he might have prevented it from becoming more lopsided than it was at the second intermission — but removing him was logical, regardless of who Sullivan turns to for Game 5.

Fleury was subjected to game-quality traffic and shots for the first time in nearly two months,

Tampa Bay's Tyler Johnson celebrates after scoring a goal in the second period to give the Lightning a 4-0 lead. The Lightning won 4-3 to tie the Eastern Conference Final at 2-2. (Peter Diana/Post-Gazette)

while Murray had an opportunity to rest.

He certainly didn't get much of that while he was in the game.

Callahan put the Lightning in front to stay just 27 seconds after the opening faceoff, as he deflected a Victor Hedman shot past Murray.

"We wanted to have a good start," Callahan said. "Obviously, when you score on the first shift, it helps."

The Penguins weathered the rest of Tampa Bay's early surge, but Lightning defenseman Andrej Sustr exploited a defensive lapse to make it 2-0 at 14:28. And when Jonathan Drouin (14:38) and Tyler Johnson (17:48) scored in the second period to put Tampa Bay up by four, putting Fleury in the game seemed like a virtual no-brainer.

Coincidentally or otherwise, however, Fleury's teammates elevated their game in the final 20 minutes, coming within a goal of forcing overtime. At the same time, Tampa Bay seemed to lose the urgency that had served it so well in the first 40 minutes.

"It's tough, when you're up by four goals, to keep your foot on the gas," Penguins left winger Chris Kunitz said.

Phil Kessel kick-started the comeback with his team-leading eighth goal of the postseason at 1:18 of the third. Evgeni Malkin scored his first in the past nine games at 11:13, and Kunitz lifted the Penguins to within one 115 seconds later.

They couldn't get the goal that would have forced overtime, though.

"Ultimately, the goal is to win the hockey game, and when you wake up in the morning, it's not how they came back and made it a game," Lightning coach Jon Cooper said.

"Ultimately, the series is 2-2." ∎

Pittsburgh's Kris Letang tangos with Tampa Bay's Brian Boyle during the second period of Game 4. Boyle and Letang exchanged words after Letang shot the puck at Lightning forward Jonathan Drouin after a whistle in his own end. Letang was assessed both a roughing and cross-checking minor. (Peter Diana/Post-Gazette)

EASTERN CONFERENCE FINAL, GAME 5

MAY 22, 2016 · PITTSBURGH, PENNSYLVANIA
LIGHTNING 4, PENGUINS 3, OT

LOSING THEIR GRIP

Deflection Goal 53 Seconds into OT Puts Penguins on the Brink

By Dave Molinari

There is a first time for almost everything, and the Penguins proved it in their 4-3 overtime loss to the Tampa Bay Lightning in Game 5 of the Eastern Conference final at Consol Energy Center.

Repeatedly.

They lost a game when leading after two periods for the first time in 2015-16.

They lost for the second time in a row for the first time since Jan. 12-15.

They lost an overtime playoff game for the first time after winning the previous three.

And, most important, they have been shoved to the cusp of elimination from the Stanley Cup playoffs for the first time this spring.

Not that they spent any time after Game 5 working on a rough draft of their concession speech.

"We've been a resilient group most of the year," left winger Chris Kunitz said.

Tampa Bay center Tyler Johnson got the game-winning goal 53 seconds into overtime, when defenseman Jason Garrison's shot from near the left dot glanced off him before eluding goalie Marc-Andre Fleury.

The Lightning, which never had a lead until Johnson scored, had forced overtime on a Nikita Kucherov wrap-around goal at 16:44 of the third period.

Fleury, making his first start since suffering a concussion March 31, stopped 21 of 25 shots, and appeared to wear down a bit as the game progressed.

"It wasn't the best I've felt in a game," he said. "I've been practicing a lot. I should have been better."

Coach Mike Sullivan declined to evaluate Fleury's play immediately after the game — "I'd rather digest it a little bit before I jump to any conclusions," he said — and gave no indication whether he will start Fleury or Matt Murray in Game 6.

Not surprisingly, Fleury's teammates were universally supportive.

"He played hard," winger Bryan Rust said. "He played well. He's a competitor. He's a leader of this team. You can't fault him at all."

Evgeni Malkin battles Matthew Carle in the first period of Game 5. Tampa Bay's 4-3 overtime win over Pittsburgh gave the Lightning a 3-2 series lead. (Matt Freed/Post-Gazette)

Fleury hardly was exempt from criticism, though. Neither was the Penguins power play, which squandered a chance to possibly put the game out of reach midway through the second period.

The Penguins were leading, 2-0, on goals by Brian Dumoulin and Patric Hornqvist when Kucherov was assessed a holding minor at 11:02.

The Penguins failed to generate a third goal, however, and 13 seconds after Kucherov returned to the ice, Tampa Bay's Alex Killorn blurred a high shot past Fleury from outside of the left dot.

"We had a chance on that one power play to get that third goal," Sullivan said. "And they score right after it."

The Lightning scored right after Killorn's goal, too. Just 70 seconds later, Kucherov beat Fleury from inside the left circle to tie the score.

Kunitz put the Penguins back in front 49.6 seconds before the second intermission with his third goal in the past three games, but the Penguins weren't able to hold off Tampa Bay in the final 20 minutes of regulation.

Whether defenseman Trevor Daley, who will miss the rest of the playoffs because of a broken ankle, could have helped them preserve the lead never will be known, but Sullivan said, "I thought our defense played a pretty good game."

It — and the rest of the team — will have to do at least that much in Game 6, or risk having the season end in a three-game tailspin.

"We've got to gather ourselves," Sullivan said. "We've got to go back at it and try to win a game." ∎

Alex Killorn's shot gets past Penguins goalie Marc-Andre Fleury in the second period to cut the Penguins' lead to 2-1. (Peter Diana/Post-Gazette)

EASTERN CONFERENCE FINAL, GAME 6

MAY 24, 2016 · TAMPA, FLORIDA
PENGUINS 5, LIGHTNING 2

PASSING THE SURVIVAL TEST

Penguins Force Game 7 after Withstanding Lightning Rally

By Dave Molinari

The Penguins talked an awfully good game in the day or so leading up to Game 6 of the Eastern Conference final. Then, they went out and played an even better one.

They defeated Tampa Bay, 5-2, at Amalie Arena — surviving a third-period surge by the Lightning in the process — to force the series to Game 7 at Consol Energy Center.

Home ice hasn't been much of an advantage for the Penguins in Game 7s — they are 2-7 in them, including losses in each of the past five — but if they produce the same kind of all-around effort they did in Game 6, they should have a reasonable chance to reach the Stanley Cup final for the fifth time in franchise history.

"You go through different experiences, and realize how hard it is to get these kinds of opportunities," Penguins center Sidney Crosby said. "As a group, we've been through a lot, and want to make the most of it."

Penguins coach Mike Sullivan started rookie goalie Matt Murray, who responded by stopping 28 of 30 shots.

That included 17 saves in the third period, much of which played out in the Penguins' end.

Murray looked a bit out of sorts early — perhaps because he faced just four shots during the first 20 minutes — but settled in as the game went along, and was his usual unflappable self when the Lightning staged a spirited late-game comeback.

"It's pretty impressive, his demeanor," Penguins center Matt Cullen said.

The Penguins dominated the first two periods, getting unanswered goals from Phil Kessel, Kris Letang and Sidney Crosby, but were forced to fend off that furious Lightning rally in the third.

"They made a push," Kessel said.

"We bent, but we didn't break."

They came pretty close, though.

Phil Kessel celebrates after scoring the Penguins' first goal in the first period. (Peter Diana/Post-Gazette)

"Maybe we didn't respond as well as we should have," winger Bryan Rust said. "But we held on."

Brian Boyle scored twice for the Lightning — the first was inadvertently deflected past Murray by Kessel — and there was genuine suspense about the outcome until Rust pulled in a lead pass from Chris Kunitz and beat Tampa Bay goalie Andrei Vasilevskiy on a breakaway at 17:52 to make it 4-2.

"That was a huge goal," said Crosby, who has scored the winner in each of the Penguins' three victories in this series.

Nick Bonino put an exclamation point on the victory by scoring into an empty net with 53.1 seconds left.

Game 6 provided something of a template for success in Game 7 as the Penguins started well, got production from their core players and received timely saves from Murray.

"We have to play a good two-way game, play the right way," Kessel said. "And hopefully, the results follow."

Of course, that doesn't mean the Lightning will play along again, the way it did for the first two periods.

"We can't spot a team like this a three-goal lead," coach Jon Cooper said.

The Penguins were more defiant than deflated after a 4-3 overtime loss in Game 5, and that attitude served them well when they were playing to keep their season alive.

"Give Pittsburgh a ton of credit for how they played and how they handled things," Cooper said.

"They volleyed the ball into our court, and now it's our turn to smash it back."

The Penguins are aware this victory only extended their season, and that a loss in Game 7 would undo whatever they accomplished in Game 6.

"We only won one game here," right winger Patric Hornqvist said.

"We're not done yet. And [Game 7's] going to be an even harder one." ■

Bryan Rust beats Tampa Bay goalie Andrei Vasilevskiy in the third period. Rust's goal gave the Penguins a 4-2 lead. (Peter Diana/Post-Gazette)

EASTERN CONFERENCE FINAL, GAME 7

MAY 26, 2016 · PITTSBURGH, PENNSYLVANIA
PENGUINS 2, LIGHTNING 1

THE STUFF OF LEGENDS
Rookie Rust Nets 2 Goals; Penguins off to Final
By Dave Molinari

Bryan Rust scored an insurance goal late in the Penguins' 5-2 victory in Game 6 of the Eastern Conference final.

Said afterward that it was the biggest goal of his career.

Probably was.

That night, anyway.

Today, it's lucky to crack the top three.

The two Rust scored in the Penguins' 2-1 victory against Tampa Bay at Consol Energy Center — goals that lifted them into the Stanley Cup final for the first time since 2009 — surely hurdled the one from a couple of nights earlier.

"That's the way you dream it up," Rust said.

While his performance might not become quite as celebrated in franchise lore as Max Talbot's two-goal effort in Game 7 of the 2009 Cup final against Detroit, it probably won't be far from it.

After all, Rust not only helped to put the Penguins back into the Cup final, but gave them their first Game 7 home-ice victory since 1995.

The Penguins' lineup features more than a few game-breakers — guys like Sidney Crosby and Evgeni Malkin and Phil Kessel — but the player who became the hero of Game 7 comes from a bit farther down the depth chart.

"I'm not sure [Rust] would have been the guy that I would have picked," coach Mike Sullivan said.

Nonetheless, he gave the Penguins a 1-0 lead at 1:55 of the second period, when he skated across the Tampa Bay blue line and took a pass from Chris Kunitz in stride before putting a shot over goalie Andrei Vasilevskiy's glove.

Thirty seconds after Jonathan Drouin pulled Tampa Bay even at 9:36 of the second, Rust scored the series-winner on a rare gaffe by Vasilevskiy, who was sensational in relief of No. 1 goalie Ben Bishop throughout the series.

Vasilevskiy failed to cover the carom of a Ben Lovejoy shot that went off the boards behind the Lightning net, and Rust jammed it past him on the short side.

"I just tried to smack it," Rust said.

It worked.

Then again, much of what the Penguins did on this night played out the way they hoped.

Bryan Rust pressures Lightning goalie Andrei Vasilevskiy during Game 7. Rust scored both Penguins goals as Pittsburgh eliminated Tampa Bay to move on to the Stanley Cup Final. (Peter Diana/Post-Gazette)

They outshot the Lightning, 39-17, and controlled play for most of the game. Still, Tampa Bay's quick-strike offense meant it was a never more than one quality chance from sending the game into overtime.

"They don't need 40 shots," Lovejoy said. "They don't need 39 to score four or five goals. They are incredibly opportunistic.

"They have some of the most elite skill in the world, and they don't need to dominate games to win. We knew we had to play smart hockey."

They made a particular point of doing that in the third period, when Tampa Bay was pressing for the tying goal.

The Penguins had become too passive late in Game 6, and the Lightning whittled a 3-0 deficit to 3-2 before Rust locked up the victory on a breakaway.

With Game 7 — and a berth in the Cup final — on the line in the final 20 minutes, the Penguins were far more assertive than they had been 48 hours earlier.

They survived all that Tampa Bay threw at them and earned the right to take on another challenge.

"We're very happy to be going where we're going," Lovejoy said.

"Now we have to focus and go out and get four more [victories]." ■

The Penguins celebrate in front of the Consol Energy Center crowd after beating the Lightning in Game 7. (Peter Diana/Post-Gazette)

STANLEY CUP PLAYOFFS '16
PENGUINS 5 RANGERS 2
EASTERN QUARTERFINAL GAME 1

Detroit silences local party

Bullpen wastes fine effort by Vogelsong

By Stephen J. Nesbitt
Pittsburgh Post-Gazette

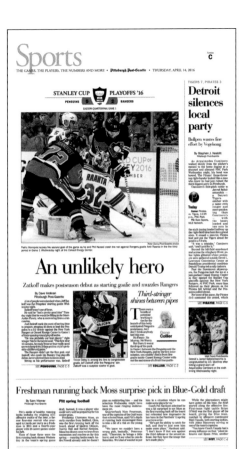

Panik, Hornqvist scores his second goal of the game as he and Phil Kessel crash the net against Rangers goalie Antti Raanta in the first period in Game 1 Wednesday night at the Consol Energy Center.

An unlikely hero

Zatkoff makes postseason debut as starting goalie and muzzles Rangers

By Dave Molinari
Pittsburgh Post-Gazette

Third-stringer shines between pipes

Gene Collier

Freshman running back Moss surprise pick in Blue-Gold draft

By Sam Werner

STANLEY CUP PLAYOFFS '16
PENGUINS 3 RANGERS 2
EASTERN QUARTERFINAL GAME 3

Cullen unlocks the door

Breakaway goal in third period gives Penguins 2-1 lead in series

By Dave Molinari
Pittsburgh Post-Gazette

Matt Cullen, left, celebrates his go-ahead goal with Ben Lovejoy and Bryan Rust. Tuesday night against the Rangers in New York. Cullen's goal broke a 2-2 tie. Story, Page E-3.

Sullivan stays hot with his decision to start Murray

Ron Cook

Pitt football | Analysis

Spring drills had some answers but others will wait for summer

By Sam Werner

PADRES 5, PIRATES 2

Liriano's control problems continue in loss to Padres

By Bill Brink

STANLEY CUP PLAYOFFS '16
PENGUINS 5 RANGERS 0
EASTERN QUARTERFINAL GAME 4

In the fast lane

Malkin gets up to speed with 4-point game

By Dave Molinari
Pittsburgh Post-Gazette

Center Evgeni Malkin celebrates his second-period goal Thursday in the 5-0 Game 4 Eastern Conference quarterfinal victory against the New York Rangers at Madison Square Garden in New York.

Pirates' Caribbean series in doubt

Players worried about exposure to Zika virus

By Bill Brink
Pittsburgh Post-Gazette

Cole delivers

Crosby is living up to his star status

Ron Cook

Drafting backup QB in middle to late rounds could happen

STANLEY CUP PLAYOFFS '16
PENGUINS 6 RANGERS 3
EASTERN QUARTERFINAL GAME 5

Return of the good vibes

Penguins get happy ending to playoff trilogy with Rangers

By Dave Molinari
Pittsburgh Post-Gazette

Brian Dumoulin, right, congratulates goalie Matt Murray moments after the Penguins eliminated the New York Rangers from the Stanley Cup playoffs with a 6-3 win in Game 5 of an Eastern Conference quarterfinal series Saturday at Consol Energy Center.

A different team slays its nemesis

Gene Collier

NFL draft still risky despite more and more information

By Ed Bouchette

DRAFT BOARD

Hitters quiet, gloves shaky as Arizona rolls to victory

By Stephen J. Nesbitt

DIAMONDBACKS 7, PIRATES 1

STANLEY CUP PLAYOFFS '16
PENGUINS 3 CAPITALS 2
EASTERN SEMIFINAL GAME 2

Fehr's goal stuns old team

Gets winner, then rookie Murray slams door on Capitals

By Dave Molinari
Pittsburgh Post-Gazette

Gene Collier

Defensive showing one to remember

Chris Kunitz, left, celebrates with Eric Fehr after Fehr scored what proved to be the winning goal late in Game 2 Saturday.

Top 3 picks could start this fall as buildup of defense continues

By Ed Bouchette

On the Steelers: NFL draft

Liriano gets back in gear, offense stays hot in the rain

By Stephen J. Nesbitt

STANLEY CUP PLAYOFFS '16
PENGUINS 3 CAPITALS 2
EASTERN SEMIFINAL GAME 3

A welcome Matt

Rookie Murray stops 47 shots; Penguins seize 2-1 series lead

By Dave Molinari
Pittsburgh Post-Gazette

Goalie Matt Murray makes one of his 47 saves Monday night against the Washington Capitals in Game 3 of the Eastern Conference semifinal series at Consol Energy Center.

Letang shouldn't be surprised if late hit results in suspension

Ron Cook

Season series begins with tension, Cole 'out of sync'

By Bill Brink

Harrison will return at OLB; no 5th-year option for Jones

By Ed Bouchette

Sports — C

STANLEY CUP PLAYOFFS '16
PENGUINS 3 — 2 CAPITALS
EASTERN SEMIFINAL GAME 4

Just call him Saint Patric

Hornqvist nets winner to end Penguins' OT skid in playoffs
By Dave Molinari — Pittsburgh Post-Gazette

Carl Hagelin flips over Capitals goalie Braden Holtby after being hit from behind Wednesday night in Game 4 at Consol Energy Center.

No Letang in lineup not a death knell for Penguins
Gene Collier

Looking ahead | U.S. Open
Spieth says Oakmont 'lived up and passed the hype' it receives
By Gerry Dulac — Pittsburgh Post-Gazette

CUBS 6, PIRATES 2
Lack of timely hits open door for Chicago's sweep
By Bill Brink — Pittsburgh Post-Gazette

Sports — F

STANLEY CUP PLAYOFFS '16
PENGUINS 4 — 3 CAPITALS
EASTERN SEMIFINAL GAME 6

It's just in the nick of time

Orpik leads Capitals into wasteland
Gene Collier

Bonino scores series winner after Washington rally forces OT
By Dave Molinari — Pittsburgh Post-Gazette

Phil Kessel celebrates the first of his two goals Tuesday that helped give the Penguins a 3-0 lead in Game 6.

ACC meetings
Coaches hear message of restraint and research on concussion issue
By Craig Meyer

Pirates
Freese eager to move across diamond into first-base role
By Bill Brink

Sports — E

STANLEY CUP PLAYOFFS '16
PENGUINS 3 — 2 LIGHTNING
EASTERN CONFERENCE FINAL GAME 2

Crosby steals the show

Matt Cullen congratulates Sidney Crosby after the latter scored the game-winning goal in overtime against the Tampa Bay Lightning in Game 2 of the Eastern Conference final Monday at Consol Energy Center.

Vasilevskiy was excellent until Crosby displays his brilliance
Gene Collier

Ends scoring drought in style with goal 40 seconds into OT
By Dave Molinari — Pittsburgh Post-Gazette

PIRATES 8, BRAVES 5
Joyce takes advantage of start, hits a homer
By Bill Brink — Pittsburgh Post-Gazette

Pine-Richland QB star commits to Notre Dame
By Mike White — Pittsburgh Post-Gazette

Sports — C

STANLEY CUP PLAYOFFS '16
PENGUINS 4 — 2 LIGHTNING
EASTERN CONFERENCE FINAL GAME 3

Shower of stars and goals

Hagelin's score late in second period opens floodgates
By Dave Molinari — Pittsburgh Post-Gazette

Patric Hornqvist, right, and Tampa Bay's Brian Boyle fight for control of the puck early in Game 3 Wednesday night in Tampa, Fla.

Murray justifies coach's decision
Ron Cook

Pitt
Return to script logo just one change at Pitt
By Craig Meyer

BRAVES 3, PIRATES 1
Teheran puts silencer on bats; Atlanta records its 10th victory
By Stephen J. Nesbitt

Sports — E

STANLEY CUP PLAYOFFS '16
PENGUINS 3 — 1 LIGHTNING
EASTERN CONFERENCE FINAL GAME 6

Passing the survival test

Half of the marbles on the line
Gene Collier

Penguins force Game 7 after withstanding Lightning rally
By Dave Molinari — Pittsburgh Post-Gazette

Phil Kessel got the Penguins on the scoreboard with his ninth goal of the postseason in the first period of Game 6 Tuesday in Tampa, Fla.

Steelers
Bell accuses Burfict, Bengals of intentionally injuring him
By Ed Bouchette — Pittsburgh Post-Gazette

PIRATES 12, DIAMONDBACKS 3
Polanco drives in 5 runs to power rout of Arizona
By Bill Brink — Pittsburgh Post-Gazette

Sports — D

STANLEY CUP PLAYOFFS '16
PENGUINS 2 — 1 LIGHTNING
EASTERN CONFERENCE FINAL GAME 7

The stuff of legends

Rookie Rust nets 2 goals; it's off to final
By Dave Molinari — Pittsburgh Post-Gazette

Winger Bryan Rust celebrates the second of his two goals against the Tampa Bay Lightning Thursday in Game 7 of the Eastern Conference final at Consol Energy Center.

Finally, a win in a Game 7 on home ice
Gene Collier

PIRATES 8, DIAMONDBACKS 3
Cole, Harrison lead sweep with key hits
By Bill Brink — Pittsburgh Post-Gazette

Brown off dance floor, schools rookie corner
By Ed Bouchette — Pittsburgh Post-Gazette

Penguins goalie Matt Murray prepares
before Game 7 of the Eastern Conference
Final. (Peter Diana/Post-Gazette)